TEST-TUBE MYSTERIES

TEST-TUBE

MYSTERIES

Gail Kay Haines

ILLUSTRATED WITH PHOTOGRAPHS

DODD, MEAD & COMPANY · NEW YORK

1 2 3 4 5 6 7 8 9 10

Library of Congress Cataloging in Publication Data

Haines, Gail Kay.
  Test-tube mysteries.

  Includes index.
  Summary: Fourteen tales describe the scientific
procedures used by a variety of scientists, including
Pasteur and George Washington Carver, to make
significant discoveries and breakthroughs in scientific
knowledge.
    1. Science—Juvenile literature.   2. Scientists—
Biography—Juvenile literature.   [1. Science.
2. Scientists]   I. Title.
Q163.H235   1982   509   82-45380
ISBN 0-396-08075-8

Contents

TEST-TUBE MYSTERIES

1 The Clue in the

Curious Crystals

It was October of 1844, and two prominent European scientists had a problem to lay before the French Académie des Sciences. They were, they admitted, completely baffled.

For several years it had been known that tartaric acid, a chemical made from the crust that forms inside wine barrels, had a peculiar effect on polarized light. Polarized light is light that has passed through a prism, so that it shines only in one flat plane, not in all directions. When polarized light shines through a solution of tartaric acid or one of its salts, the light always comes out with its plane slightly rotated to the right, like a spoke on a turning wheel.

Tartaric acid was important for making medicines and sparkling water in those days, and several factories had been built to produce it. One of those factories occasionally found some sharp, needlelike crystals growing among the thicker crystals of tartaric acid. Because they looked a little different, these crystals were called paratartaric acid, or sometimes racemic acid, from the Latin word for grape.

Eilhardt Mitscherlich, a well-known German chemist, began to study the two kinds of crystals. They seemed to be crystals of exactly the same thing.

Mitscherlich used every chemical test he knew and could not find a way to tell tartaric from paratartaric acid, once they had been dissolved in water. Except one. A solution of paratartaric acid did not rotate polarized light, and tartaric acid did.

Mitscherlich sent a description of his experiments, with samples of the chemicals, to his friend Jean Baptiste Biot. Biot was an elderly French chemist and a member of the Académie. He tried the same experiments, plus a few of his own. The results were the same. Biot could not tell the two acids apart, unless he looked at their solutions through a special instrument called a polarimeter. Then, always, the beam of light polarized by the prism inside the instrument rotated to the right for one and stayed the same for the other.

Biot was puzzled. How could two chemicals be so much alike and yet have a difference? And what, exactly, was the difference? No one knew.

Louis Pasteur was not a member of the Académie des Sciences in 1844, so he was not present the night Biot read a note from Mitscherlich to the Académie, outlining the mystery. Pasteur was a hard-working twenty-two-year-old chemistry student at the École Normale in Paris.

Pasteur read Mitscherlich's note in the school library. It fascinated him. He loved chemical mysteries.

But Pasteur was too busy earning his degree in chemistry to have much time for curious crystals. Besides, how could he discover what famous chemists such as Mitscherlich and Biot could not? He put the problem to the back of his mind.

Louis Pasteur

Two years later, Pasteur graduated and went to work in a chemical laboratory at the same school. In his spare time, he began exploring the mystery. Tartatic acid crystals were beautiful and easy to grow. Pasteur prepared sample after sample of the acid and its different salts.

Some of the young chemist's regular work dealt with crystals, and he began to learn some interesting facts about them. Crystals grow on each other and stick together like chunks of rock candy, so it is not easy to determine the shape of individual crystals. But Pasteur knew that each kind of crystal has its own, characteristic form.

Pasteur studied clumps of tartaric acid crystals under a microscope, patiently sorting and inspecting and sometimes prying them apart with a needle. He soon began to see distinct shapes and, almost at once, Pasteur observed something Mitscherlich had never reported. The crystals were not symmetrical. Each had an extra facet, or face, on one side, and it was always the same side. It was as if each crystal were "right-handed," like a mitten with the thumb sticking out.

Pasteur was elated. To think the problem was so simple! Now he began to prepare samples of paratartaric acid salts, certain that he would find no "thumb," or extra facet, on crystals of the chemical which did not rotate polarized light.

When the microscope was steadied, Pasteur stirred the crystals of paratartaric acid loose from each other and inspected them. He felt a surge of disappointment. The separate crystals looked just like the other ones. Each single crystal had a "thumb." In his own words, "For an instant, my heart stopped beating."

Pasteur could have given up then. He had been so sure the shape of the crystals would be the answer.

But Pasteur did not give up. Looking closely into the lens,

he suddenly realized that the crystals were not quite all alike, after all. Some of them were "right-handed," as before, but others had the extra facet on the other side. They were "left-handed" crystals, mirror images of the first kind, the way a pair of mittens are mirror images of each other. The paratartaric acid was a mixture of the two kinds, while tartaric acid had only "rights."

"Tout est trouvé!" Pasteur is said to have shouted. "All is found out!"

Now the young French chemist began to do what no one had ever done before. Slowly, he pushed a needle among the tiny crystals under his microscope, studying each one carefully and scooting the "right-handed" ones to one side and the "left-handed" ones to the other. Soon he had two piles.

When he had dissolved both piles of paratartaric acid crystals separately in water, Pasteur passed a beam of polarized light through each. He looked into his polarimeter. The solution of "right-handed" crystals rotated the beam to the right, exactly as tartaric acid did. The "left-handed" half rotated light, too, but this time the beam moved to the left. A mixture of the two did not rotate light at all.

Pasteur had discovered a third substance, with "left-handed" crystals, hidden in the paratartaric acid, and he had solved Mitscherlich's mystery. Finally, he could explain the difference between the two almost identical acids. Tartaric acid has all "right-handed" crystals, but paratartaric has a mixture. Pasteur was so excited that he ran out into the hall and grabbed the first person he met, to show off his results.

But Pasteur's troubles were not over yet. It was now 1848, and he was a graduate chemist, but he was not very well known. When he reported his discovery to the Académie des Sciences, most of the noted scientists did not believe him. They could not decide whether he was trying to fool them, or was simply confused.

To settle the matter, Biot, who had introduced the mystery to the Académie, invited Pasteur to the laboratory in his own home. He greeted the young chemist formally, and offered to provide all the materials Pasteur would need, so there could be no question of fraud. Under Biot's eye, Pasteur prepared another batch of samples.

It took two days for the crystals to grow. A nervous Pasteur returned home and waited for Biot to send word that the crystals were ready.

Back in Biot's laboratory, Pasteur carefully sorted the crystals. He dissolved them and handed both samples to Biot, who chose the "left-handed" sample first.

When the elderly chemist looked into his own polarimeter and saw crystals from his own sample of paratartaric acid rotating light to the left, he was convinced at last. In fact, he was so excited that he flung his arms around Pasteur and exclaimed, "My dear boy, my whole life has been devoted to science. What I have just seen makes my old heart beat faster."

The clue in the curious crystals led to a lifelong friendship between the young Pasteur and the famous Biot. And, eventually, this and other important discoveries made Louis Pasteur far more famous than any of the scientists who had doubted him.

Solving the mystery also led to the beginning of a whole new field of chemistry called stereochemistry, the study of the shapes of molecules. Learning how molecules and the crystals they form are put together has led to the development of many useful chemicals which never existed before.

2 The Secret in the Sticky Test Tube

Sometimes, in mystery books, a teenage detective tackles an almost unsolvable problem. He goes about it in all the wrong ways. He comes up with an impossible answer—which "just happens" to be the solution to a completely different mystery. That plot was originated by a teenage chemist named William Perkin, more than one hundred years ago.

Coal was big business in England in the 1850s. Giant factories turned the black, lumpy fuel into easy-to-burn coal gas and coke. But the factories had a problem. Leftover coal tar kept building mountains in their backyards.

The smelly, sticky black tar wasn't good for much of anything. Factory owners didn't know what to do with it. The gummy waste material was more of a nuisance than a mystery, but no one could think of a solution to the problem.

Then Queen Victoria's husband, Prince Albert, invited August Wilhelm von Hofmann to start a chemistry department at the Royal College of Science. The German chemist had heard about the mountains of unwanted tar, and he had thought of

15

a few ideas for using it up. Hofmann and some of his students began distilling chemicals from the sticky tar.

Until tragedy struck. One of the chemical-making stills caught fire, and a student died of burns. That cooled the enthusiasm of Hofmann's other students for finding ways to use coal tar. Tar was not just a nuisance, it was a hazard.

Except William Perkin. William was more interested in coal tar than ever, because he had a fantastic idea. If it worked, his idea could turn coal tar into a useful product, save thousands of lives, and make William rich and famous, all at the same time. It was a chemist's dream, and William could hardly wait for a chance to put his plan into action.

But life as a student wasn't easy. The German professor kept William so busy he had no time to do any experimenting on his own.

So William waited. He hated waiting.

William Perkin had always been impatient to get his career started. First, he followed his builder-father around building sites, imitating the carpenters. Then he discovered a book on engineering and set out to build his own full-sized locomotive (he couldn't get all the parts he needed). Next, he decided on a career in oil painting.

Finally, a friend demonstrated some chemical experiments. William was fascinated. "I saw there was in chemistry something far beyond other pursuits," he said later. "My choice was fixed." All this happened before William was thirteen years old.

William immediately began collecting bottles and chemicals to set up a laboratory at home. He gave up lunches to hear lectures on chemistry, since the science was not in the curriculum at his school.

Courtesy of the Edgar Fahs Smith Collection

William Perkin, as an old man

In two years he had learned enough to enter the Royal College of Science, and in two more years he had become Professor Hofmann's main assistant. At seventeen, he felt ready to tackle any kind of chemical problem.

Easter vacation, 1856, gave William the chance he had been waiting for. He still had his laboratory at home, and there was plenty of coal tar available. The young chemist set to work on his own, special idea—making quinine out of coal tar.

In the mid-nineteenth century, thousands of Englishmen and their families lived in India. And every year, hundreds of them died. One of the most serious killer-diseases in India was malaria, which infected almost everyone, British and Indian, alike. The only drug which could save them was quinine.

Quinine does not cure malaria, but it can control it. Malaria victims had to swallow dose after dose of the bitter medicine, sometimes every day for years. So, naturally, England needed huge amounts of quinine. And quinine could only be made from the bark of the South American cinchona tree.

William overheard Professor Hofmann talking about quinine, and how rich the discoverer of artificial, inexpensive quinine would become. William planned to be that discoverer.

He studied the drug in the lab, and soon William knew as much about its chemical makeup as any other chemist of his day. It was formed from quite ordinary ingredients—all of them found in coal tar.

Allyltoluidine, one of the chemicals Hofmann's students had discovered in coal tar, seemed to be made from almost exactly the same atoms as quinine, but only about half as many per molecule. The biggest difference was that quinine had more oxygen in its makeup.

That gave William his exciting idea. If he could get two molecules of allyltoluidine to join together, picking up extra oxygen from some potassium chromate (which was known for giving off oxygen to other compounds), he might get quinine. And coal tar was certainly cheaper than tree bark from South America!

In his makeshift lab at home, William mixed and heated the two chemicals. He knew what quinine looked like—clear, needlelike crystals. But instead of shiny crystals, he created a gummy, reddish-brown mess in the bottom of his test tube. It wouldn't crystallize, it wouldn't dissolve, it wouldn't even wash out.

Chemists in William's day were mainly interested in crystals. They thought sticky substances were as worthless as coal tar, and they normally threw them out.

But William couldn't throw away the mysterious goo. It was stuck fast to the glass.

Intrigued, William decided to try again. This time, he chose a simpler coal tar chemical called aniline. William heated the strong-smelling yellow liquid with more potassium chromate in a clean glass tube.

And this time, instead of a brownish, sticky mess, he got a blackish, sticky mess. No crystals, no quinine, no fame or fortune. His only discovery was some ugly goo which had ruined two test tubes. William almost tossed the whole mess into the trash.

The trouble was, William's idea was dead wrong. Quinine may be made from the same elements as the chemicals William was using, but its structure is so complex that it would be another fifty years before any chemist could puzzle it out and a hundred years before anyone would be able to synthesize it.

Fortunately, William didn't know that what he was doing was impossible. And more fortunately, he didn't throw his failure away.

What William *did* do next is told in several ways. Some historians say he held the second tube up to a window and caught a glint of color. Others write that he simply wanted to get his test tubes clean.

For whatever reason, William Perkin poured alcohol into the residue from his quinine-making venture. And in the second tube, the black muck dissolved into a beautiful purple liquid.

Now the test tube washed clean and clear. But when he splashed the colorful chemical onto fabric, it left a permanent lilac stain. William had failed to solve the problem of making quinine, but he had found a clue to a mystery hundreds of years older. He had unlocked the door to the world of artificial color.

Dye had always mystified chemists. For centuries, scientists had been hunting an inexpentive way to brighten clothing. But any colors they managed to create quickly faded or washed away.

It seemed that only certain plants and animals could produce permanent, colorful dyes. Tyrian purple, for instance, came from a complex and expensive process involving tiny sea snails from the Mideast. No wonder "born to the purple" meant "born wealthy"!

In William's day, color was only for the rich. Yet, unbelievably, William held in his hand a tube of the prettiest, brightest color he had ever seen, and it had cost him almost nothing.

William had trouble convincing the world that he had solved a problem which had eluded all the older and wiser chemists for centuries. He had the most trouble convincing his father, especially when he wanted to quit school and go into the dye business.

But William's dye spoke for itself. Soon almost everyone in Europe was wearing the color William named "mauveine." It was not long before other chemists were discovering other synthetic dyes from the chemicals in coal tar, but William's was first and, for a long time, the best.

Financially, mauveine was a spectacular success. William Perkin became rich and famous beyond his wildest plans. The king made him Sir William Henry Perkin.

And as soon as his industrial empire was well established, William retired and went back to his laboratory. Doing chemical experiments, he felt, was more important than making money. And more fun.

William's find started the whole petrochemical synthetics industry which provides most of the material modern society needs to thrive. One inquisitive teenager, from a clue in a sticky test tube, helped bring chemistry out of the laboratory and into everyone's life.

3 The Baffling Bubble

Mystery

The first mysterious bubble appeared when Henry Cavendish decided to investigate air. The year was 1785. The place, an old, isolated mansion outside London, England.

Air was causing a sensation in the chemical world. For centuries, everyone had thought air was an element, a basic, undividable kind of matter. Then, European scientists found a way to take air apart. It seemed to be made of two colorless gases, "oxygen" and "nitrogen."

Alone in his private laboratory, Henry Cavendish rechecked all their experiments, looking for errors. At first, he couldn't find any.

Oxygen was fun to study. Candles burned brightly in it, mice frisked around in a beaker of it, and it felt exhilarating to breathe.

Nitrogen, on the other hand, didn't do much of anything. Candles snuffed their flames in it, mice died, and it had no taste or smell.

According to all the reports Cavendish had read, air was ⅕

oxygen. Chemists let the active gas react with some other chemical, measured it, and then measured what air was left. Since
they couldn't get the remaining ⅘ of air to react with anything,
they called it all nitrogen.

This made Henry Cavendish suspicious. He didn't trust other
scientists' reports. How can they be sure air is ⅘ nitrogen? he
wondered. What if something else is in there? He decided to
find a way to make the unreactive nitrogen react, so he could
see for himself.

Henry Cavendish did all his own lab work. He never met or
talked with other scientists, or any other men if he could avoid
it. (And as for women, Henry refused to speak to them at all.
He left notes for his cook, telling her what to serve for dinner.)

At first, none of his experiments on nitrogen worked. The
inert gas refused to react with anything.

But nitrogen *could* combine with other elements, Henry
knew, because nature abounds with nitrogen-containing compounds. The lazy gas just needed something extra to force it
to start.

Then Henry Cavendish got an idea. Scientists knew enough
about electricity two hundred years ago to make sparks jump
from wire to wire. And when Henry passed a series of sparks
through a container of air, reactions began happening.

When he bubbled the same air through water, ¼ of it disappeared. Some nitrogen and oxygen had changed into something that dissolved in water.

But most of the air was still left. That wasn't too disturbing.
There is so much more nitrogen than oxygen in air that the
reaction must have run out of oxygen. Sure enough, when
Henry bubbled pure oxygen into the container and sparked it

again, almost all the air disappeared.

But not quite all. After every bit of extra oxygen had been removed and all the nitrogen had reacted, there was something left. A tiny, colorless bubble, about $\frac{1}{120}$ of the starting amount, floated above the water.

Some mysterious gas, even more unreactive than nitrogen, seemed to be hidden in air. Cavendish tried all the techniques of his day, but he couldn't change the bubble, get rid of it, or learn any more about it. The bubble just sat there.

Most scientists would have announced the discovery of a new gas to the world. Not Henry Cavendish. He wrote a paper about the strange bubble, but he didn't bother to publicize it.

The bubble was clue number one to a major mystery, but it lay buried for more than a century. Henry Cavendish died long before it was solved.

Clue number two appeared when Pierre Janssen investigated an eclipse of the sun. The year was 1868. The place, an observation post in India.

Pierre Janssen loved eclipses. The French astronomer followed them all over the world, even escaping by balloon from a war-occupied city in time to catch a ship to the next location. He made several important discoveries while he was in India, but one observation proved to be a mystery.

Janssen was using instruments to study the sun after the eclipse, when he and five other astronomers came across a strange reading. It was a yellow line where no line ought to be.

For several years, scientists had been experimenting with a new tool called a spectroscope. Put simply, a spectroscope breaks down light into lines and bands the way a prism breaks sunlight into a rainbow. Every chemical element, when heated to glow-

Courtesy of the Edgar Fahs Smith Collection

Henry Cavendish

ing, gives off (or absorbs) a different "fingerprint" pattern of lights and colors.

The spectroscope had helped chemists discover several new elements, when unexpected sets of lines appeared. But the researchers had always been able to follow up the "discovery" by taking the glowing substance apart, chemically, to find the new element hidden inside. The scope simply showed them where to look.

This time, things were more complicated. The astronomers had found a new line in sunlight's "fingerprint." How could they analyze the sun?

Pierre Janssen was not a chemist. He couldn't figure out what the odd line meant, so he left it out of his report.

But the scientist couldn't forget that mysterious line. He shipped his data to an expert on spectroscopes—Sir Joseph Norman Lockyer, in England.

Sir Joseph knew right away what the line meant. It had to be a new element. Possibly it was something found only on the sun. He named it "helium," meaning "metal of the sun."

No one took the discovery seriously. In fact, other scientists laughed at Sir Joseph. They thought he was crazy to put real faith in a light-splitting gadget. Before they would believe in helium, most people wanted solid evidence. Unfortunately, he didn't have any.

Clue number three surfaced when Luigi Palmieri investigated a volcano. The year: 1881. The place: Mount Vesuvius Observatory, Italy.

The same yellow line appeared as Luigi Palmieri spectroscoped some white, crusty material from the crater rim of Mount Vesuvius. A few bubbles of gas escaped, and they had spectral "fingerprints" to match Lockyer's helium. But this clue slipped by unnoticed.

Clue number four bubbled out when William Hillebrand investigated pitchblende. The year: 1888. The place: a geological survey station in the United States.

William Hillebrand happened to be boiling some chunks of uranium ore in acid when he noticed a string of bubbles escaping from the blackish rock. Rocks often have gases trapped inside, so the geochemist was not surprised. He decided to catch the bubbles and try to identify them.

Hillebrand set up a glass tube to catch bubbles as they boiled off. When he had a tubeful of gas, he began to analyze it. The gas didn't react with acid or base of any of the other chemicals William tried. Any gas that unreactive had to be nitrogen!

To be certain, Hillebrand used a spectroscope. As expected, the spectral lines for nitrogen appeared. There were some extra lines, too. William didn't know what they were, so he didn't bother about them.

Then he tried passing an electrical current through the sample of gas. Most of the gas disappeared, dissolving into the water at the bottom of the container, exactly as nitrogen should.

But there was still one tiny bubble left. No matter how hard he tried, William could not get that bubble to dissolve. So he ignored it.

William Hillebrand wrote a scientific report on his discovery of trapped nitrogen in pitchblende. He mentioned the extra spectral lines and the mysterious final bubble, but he didn't try to explain them. He didn't think they were important.

The next clue appeared when a famous British nobleman decided to investigate a new theory about atoms. The year was

1892. The location, Terling Place, an ancestral mansion not far from London.

Lord Rayleigh, whose name was John William Strutt, had never heard of a "bubble mystery." He was not at all interested in chemistry, but he was expert at facts and figures. In his private physics laboratory, he was working on a problem which required careful and perfectly precise measurements.

Some scientists were convinced that all atoms are made of different numbers of hydrogen atoms, locked together. That made sense, because hydrogen is the smallest and lightest atom. If so, each atom ought to be an even multiple of the weight of hydrogen. But was it or wasn't it?

Atoms are much too tiny to weigh individually. Most scientists settled for measuring the same volume of different gases and dividing the weight by the number of atoms calculated to be inside. It was not easy, and different scientists came out with slightly different answers.

Lord Rayleigh determined to solve the problem by doing the best, most accurate job possible. He spent ten years making certain he had the weights of hydrogen and oxygen perfectly correct.

If the theory were right, oxygen atoms should weigh exactly eight times as much as hydrogen atoms. But they didn't, quite.

Then Rayleigh tackled nitrogen. And there, the bubble mystery resurfaced.

Lord Rayleigh's system had been to collect a gas from several different sources, measure each, and make sure the results agreed. With hydrogen and oxygen, they always did.

But with nitrogen, they didn't. Every time he produced nitro-

Lord Rayleigh

gen from chemicals, he got one answer. And every time he collected nitrogen from air, he got another. Every single time!

The two conflicting weights frustrated the baron. In fact, they almost drove him crazy. He was being impeccably careful, but the results refused to agree. No matter how often he redid his experiment, the sample of N_2 taken from air weighed out 0.1 percent heavier.

Some scientists would have ignored so small a difference. In fact, they had been ignoring it for years. It only amounted to one part in a thousand.

But perfect accuracy was the whole point of his experiment. How could the famous physicist announce to the world that other atoms are definitely not made from hydrogen when his own figures did not agree?

Something was wrong, but what? If it was not his work— and Lord Rayleigh was sure it was not—then it had to be something else. The baron admitted he was stumped.

Finally, in September, 1892, he wrote a letter to *Nature* explaining his predicament. Could anyone help?

Nature was the top scientific magazine of the day, and everyone who cared about science read it. But no one answered the letter. For over a year, there was not one response.

Professor William Ramsay stumbled onto the mystery when he read Lord Rayleigh's letter, but he ignored it. The answer looked easy to guess—Lord Rayleigh must have made a mistake. The time: 1892. The place: University of London.

Then, months later, Ramsay heard the famous baron speak at a meeting, and he changed his mind. For one thing, everyone knew and respected the physicist as a careful worker who did

Courtesy of the Edgar Fahs Smith Collection

William Ramsay

not make many mistakes. For another thing, Ramsay had just had a flash of memory.

Men on both sides of Ramsay's family were chemists, but William "discovered" chemistry in his last year of college. Laid up with a broken leg from playing football, he picked up a chemistry book to see how fireworks were made. By the end of the term, he and a friend had turned William's bedroom into a laboratory full of bottles and flasks and chemical smells. They worked in it every afternoon, after classes.

But William liked reading about chemistry almost as much as he liked doing experiments. And most of what he read stayed in his head. That's where he got the idea for solving Lord Rayleigh's mystery.

Years before, another scientist had published some of Henry Cavendish's century-old notes. The notes described a mysterious, unidentified bubble found in air. William had written "look into this" in the margin of the book and then forgotten about it. But if there were really an undiscovered substance hiding in air, it could be causing all Lord Rayleigh's problems.

William Ramsay was only a professor at a small university, while the famous baron-scientist was secretary of the Royal Society of London for the Improvement of Natural Knowledge. Ramsay didn't dare meddle in Lord Rayleigh's project without permission.

He wrote to the baron, asking if it would be all right to experiment with nitrogen from the air. Lord Rayleigh gladly agreed.

Working separately, the two scientists took the "nitrogen" sample apart. Rayleigh, the physicist, redid Cavendish's experiment with electricity. He found the same, leftover bubble.

Ramsay, the chemist, passed his sample back and forth over hot magnesium. It was a reaction Cavendish had not known about, but it pulled nitrogen gas out of the sample and turned it into a yellowish solid. Finally, only one colorless bubble was left.

William blew a glass tube and sealed the bubble in it. He viewed the tiny sample of gas through his spectroscope. The lines of nitrogen showed through; the sample wasn't quite pure yet. But strongest of all were several red and green lines no one had ever seen before. They were the spectral "fingerprint" of a new element.

Rayleigh and Ramsay pooled their information and announced the discovery jointly at the August, 1894, meeting of the Royal Society. They named the new gas "argon," meaning "lazy one." As a chemical, it was even lazier than nitrogen.

But not everyone accepted the discovery. Quite a few members of the Society were skeptical. They still had trouble accepting spectral lines as real evidence of anything.

Most confusing of all, solving the "bubble mystery" by calling it a new element merely opened a new mystery. By 1894, all the known chemical elements fitted neatly in groups on a periodic chart, according to weight and chemical activity. There was absolutely no gap for a colorless, odorless gas that didn't do anything! The scientists laughed at Ramsay's suggestion that argon might belong to a whole new group.

William Ramsay went back to work, trying to find ways to convince the doubters. Then he got a letter that made the problem easier. A friend wrote to him about Hillebrand's bubbles.

Ramsay didn't waste a minute. As soon as he finished reading the article, he sent a laboratory aide to visit all the stores in London selling minerals, buying whatever uranium ore he could find.

The assistant was back by noon with three shillings sixpence worth of an ore called cleveite. By evening they had collected several glass tubes of clear, colorless bubbles.

Now the chemists stopped rushing and began to work very carefully. They spent two days removing every trace of every gas that might contaminate the sample. What was left was colorless, odorless, and totally unreactive.

Ramsay got his spectroscope ready. Assistants and spectators crowded in as he set up an arrangement so that everyone could see a spectrum of argon and the spectrum of the "new" gas at the same time. They all expected to see bright red and green lines from the new gas overlap argon's red and green "fingerprint."

Instead, the gas produced, in William's words, "A magnificent yellow line, brilliantly bright." Surprise filled the room. "I was puzzled," Ramsay said later, "but [I] began to smell a rat."

Someone suggested that the glass tube might be dirty. Ordinary sodium also produces a yellow line. Maybe some salt (sodium chloride) had contaminated the glass.

William knew the tube was clean. After all, he had blown it himself. But as proof, he brought a tube of sodium to the scope. The yellow lines did not match.

To solve the puzzle, Professor Ramsay sent a tube of the gas to Sir William Crookes, who had built the finest spectroscope in England. His answer arrived by telegram the next Saturday morning. The strange bubble's yellow line perfectly matched astronomer Janssen's mysterious "metal of the sun." Instead of more argon, Ramsay had discovered the first recognized helium on earth.

Now William Ramsay had two new elements, both colorless gases and both completely unreactive. His "whole new group" on the chart of the elements was beginning to make more sense.

Helium was very light, and argon much heavier. If his hunch was right, another gas between them in weight should exist.

But where should he search for it? Clues from all over the world, including the sun, had helped locate the first two. Now what?

History was no further help. To finish solving the mystery, Ramsay needed something new. And he found it in a special machine.

The most exciting scientific "gadget" since the spectroscope had just been invented. It was a pump that could remove enough heat to liquify air and even freeze parts of it solid. A special kind of Thermos bottle called a cryostat kept the chilled air cold. And as the air froze and thawed, it separated into parts.

William Ramsay and his assistant, William Travers, chilled tons of air. In it, they found three more small "mystery bubbles." But the new bubbles were not mysteries for long. The two chemists found telltale spectroscopic lines of another new element in each one.

The lightest new gas, named "neon" for "the new one," lit up with brilliant light when they passed electric current through it. "A blaze of crimson light told its own story," Travers wrote later. "And it was a sight never to forget."

Neon's weight fell between helium and argon, just where Ramsay had expected. Krypton and xenon were progressively heavier.

With five new gases, the group Ramsay had predicted appeared complete. But it wasn't, quite. The final clue was one more bubble.

Radioactivity had been discovered at about the same time as the new family of gases, and it wasn't long before scientists began noticing mysterious radioactive bubbles emanating from radioactive rocks. When William Ramsay managed to collect enough of the bubbles to test, he found radon, his sixth and final gas. The baffling bubble mystery was solved by the unveiling of a whole new family of elements.

In 1904, Ramsay and Rayleigh each received a Nobel Prize— Rayleigh in Physics and Ramsay in Chemistry—for the discovery of the noble gases (called "noble" because they are so unreactive). The gases have a long list of uses, from helium balloons to neon lights.

But their discovery gave chemistry a side benefit. Instead of spoiling the periodic chart by adding an element that didn't fit, Ramsay proved its truth with a perfectly fitting new group. It was like finding the last six border pieces to a puzzle.

And Ramsay's methods taught scientists everywhere an important lesson. The more they know about the past, present, and future of science, the better their chances of solving the mysteries around them.

4 The Great Peanut

Puzzle

In A. Conan Doyle's mystery books, desperate people came from all over England to lay their problems before Sherlock Holmes. He always solved his cases by outthinking everyone else.

In "The Great Peanut Puzzle," farmers from all over Alabama brought a life-and-death problem to the smartest man they knew. His ideas often sounded crazy, but they always worked. Until now.

The first mystery George Washington Carver found when he arrived at Tuskegee Institute in 1876 was: where is the laboratory? He had been hired to teach agricultural science at a new Alabama college for black students. There seemed to be plenty of students, but very little college.

George walked around, noting the acres of bare, rutted dirt stretching in all directions, with no grass, no trees, and no crops. He smelled the pigpens and watched the turkey buzzards dive in and out of a huge rubbish heap, but he couldn't find the laboratory. There was no laboratory.

In place of the well-equipped lab and greenhouse at Iowa

State Agricultural College, where he had been teaching, Carver acquired one bare room in a delapidated building—to live in as well as work in—and twenty acres of dirt so poor it could barely grow weeds.

The handful of students assigned to work with Dr. Carver worked under protest. Farming, to them, meant hopeless drudgery. They would rather study almost anything else.

Born a slave, George Carver had been on his own since he was ten years old. He knew how to make do and do without. He also knew how to make the best of almost any situation.

Carver sent his students scouring through the trash heap at school and through dumps all over town. He had them asking at doors for cast-off pans and bottles, wire, string, and can lids, rubber, and glass or almost anything that might possibly be useful. He even sent the boys for armloads of reeds from the swamp.

With this pile of junk in an empty room, Carver solved his first mystery. He "found" a laboratory. One old lamp served to heat and melt samples, to light his microscope (a gift from his friends in Iowa), and as a hand warmer on cold mornings. Broken bottles became test tubes and beakers, once he showed students how to give them a clean edge with a burning string. Stalks of hollow reeds took the place of glass pipettes, and he used an old flatiron to pound chunks of rock and dirt into powder to study.

Working from this cluttered room, Carver started on the second, more confusing mystery: what to do about the overwhelming poverty and ignorance and hopelessness all around him.

Cotton was king in Alabama, as it was all over the South.

George Washington Carver

Scraggly stalks of cotton grew in almost every field, even up to the walls of the farmers' shacks.

But growing cotton, Carver knew, is hard on the soil. It takes out nutrients and puts nothing back.

Most of the small farm owners, black and white, were too poor to buy fertilizer. They just kept planting cotton, year after year, harvesting smaller and poorer crops each time. But they were not interested in advice from any northern scientist, especially a black northern scientist. What could he know about raising cotton?

So he showed them. On his twenty farmed-out acres, Carver helped his students plant cowpeas, which take nitrogen from the air and put it back into the soil. He had them carry muck from the swamp and spread it as fertilizer over the barren land. And he started a giant compost heap, using every scrap of organic waste he and his students could scrounge for miles around.

Carver and his students raised a crop of cotton on their "hopeless" land that produced five times more cotton fiber per acre than any other farm in the area. Black and white Alabamians came from all over the countryside just to stare at the bushy stalks.

After that, slowly, the people began to listen to and trust the teacher from "up north." They took his advice about everything from eating tomatoes (everyone had thought they were poisonous) to decorating their homes with paint made from Alabama clay.

But almost no one was ready to take his advice about giving up cotton. The more he talked about "resting the fields" and raising other kinds of produce, the more grimly they hung onto the only crop they knew someone would buy.

Disaster changed their minds. Trouble had been creeping up from Texas across the South for several years, and in 1915 it hit Alabama. The boll weevil burrowed its way into the cotton crop and ate its way out, as the stalks of cotton turned yellow, withered, and died. The destructive little beetles had killed the one crop upon which everyone's life depended.

Carver saw the deadly insects coming. He tried to get ready, but there was not much that could be done. The only hope was turning to another crop.

But what? Carver thought of sweet potatoes. Many farmers already grew them in small amounts, but they didn't seem like a cash crop. He experimented with soybeans, from China. They grew well and had plenty of uses, but they were totally strange to the southern farmer. Finally, he settled on the peanut.

Peanuts had been brought to North America by slave traders looking for the cheapest way to feed their victims. Many farmers already had a few vines growing around the house, for their children to pick and eat. It sounded perfect.

Peanuts could be roasted and eaten by the handful, but that was not nearly all. As Carver experimented in the kitchen, he learned more than a hundred ways to cook and eat peanuts. He even engineered a dinner party, cooked by the girls from the Home Economics department. The girls served soup, mock chicken, a creamed vegetable, bread, salad, ice cream, cookies, candy, and coffee. No one guessed that every single dish, including the coffee, was made mostly from peanuts.

People took Carver's advice. Hadn't he always been right before?

Soon the soft-shelled underground nuts (which are really a kind of bean) were growing all through eastern Alabama down to the Florida border. Carver was elated. His plan to save the farmer was working.

But the problems were just beginning. One day in October, an elderly widow knocked timidly on Carver's door. She asked the embarrassing question farmers all over the area were beginning to ask. "Who will buy my peanuts?" The third and deadliest mystery had arrived, and Carver had no ready answer.

The problem was too many peanuts for too small a market. No one bought them for anything but roasting, and there were tons going to waste. What to do was a mystery—and a matter of life and death for the farmers. George Carver knew peanuts were valuable. But how could he prove it?

At first, he was stumped. So he went for a walk.

All his life, George had loved going out into the woods at dawn to look at plants and to talk to God. This time, as the scientist described it years later, he wanted to talk to God about peanuts.

As the story goes, he first asked God to tell him why the universe was made. God answered that he wanted to know too much. So he asked why man was made. That was still too much. Finally, Carver asked, "Mr. Creator, why did you make the peanut?"

"That's better!" the Lord is said to have replied. And, as George Carver always told the story, he and God went into the laboratory together, to get to work.

Professor Carver had a well-equipped laboratory by this time, in a newer and larger building. But most of the old vinegar jars and sawed-off bottles and bent saucepans from that first make-shift lab were still in use. George never threw anything useful away.

Carver locked the door of "God's Little Workshop," as the students had nicknamed the new lab, with several bushels of peanuts inside. The mystery was how to make them valuable.

He thought a minute, first. Every plant is made from chemicals, combined by nature. In a chemical lab those chemicals can be taken apart and put together in new ways. Carver set out to remodel the peanut.

Wearing his old flour-sack apron, Carver shelled a handful of peanuts. His long fingers carefully separated and saved every scrap.

First, he ground the nuts to a fine, floury powder. He heated the powder and put it into a handpress. Oil began to drip out. Squeezing harder, he collected more than a cup of clear, golden oil.

Carver experimented with the oil until he had separated it into its chemical parts. He felt a thrill of excitement. This oil was special.

Most of the oil in Carver's day came from animal fat. It had a tough, jellylike coating on the oil particles, which made it hard to mix with other things. Peanut oil, without the coating, was smooth and quick-mixing.

Carver began thinking of ways to use the new easy-blending oil. He made soap and a few kinds of cosmetics. He tried rubbing it on his skin. He used it to fry other foods. In every way, it seemed superior to lard or animal tallow. Carver filled a row of little bottles with his new products.

Next, he picked up the cake of leftover peanut meal and rubbed it through his fingers. He blended it with water, warmed it, and cooled it, and flavored it with a little salt and sugar until he had a pitcher of creamy, good-tasting "milk."

The "milk" tasted so delicious he drank about half of the

first batch. But Carver was working as a chemist, not a cook. Just tasting good was not enough. He tested the "milk" and all the other food products carefully, to see what they contained. Peanut milk and, in fact, most of the food products turned out to be as wholesome and rich in protein and vitamins as the foods they imitated.

Separating the different chemicals into jars, Carver investigated shoe polish, ink, dye, shaving cream, metal polish, axle grease, and even shampoo.

He made paper from the thin red skin found between a peanut and its hull. And from the broken hulls, he made insulating board, soil conditioner, and even a hard, shiny imitation marble.

For the first few days, George Carver did not leave the laboratory. He opened the door only to take in more peanuts. He refused the meals students set outside his door. When he got hungry, he ate a handful of peanuts or taste-tested one of his edible products.

By the end of the first week, Carver had developed more than a dozen useful, salable products that could be made from peanuts. Over the next few years he brought the list to over three hundred.

Businessmen were quick to make use of his findings. And since Carver refused to patent or take money for any of his discoveries, the ideas could be put into immediate use.

The peanuts were ready, and labor was available. It was not long before factories began to appear, making products from peanuts and making money for the farmers and the manufacturers and the whole South. Carver had solved the mystery in a very profitable way—for everyone but himself. (That didn't matter to George Carver. Most of the time he didn't even bother to cash his paychecks.)

When the U.S. entered World War I and foreign supplies and products became difficult to get, Carver's synthetic peanut-products became more and more important. Peanuts eventually became the second leading cash crop in the South, and one of the six leading crops in the United States.

In 1919, the people of Alabama built a monument to the boll weevil, in joking appreciation of what it had done for the economy by driving the farmers into raising peanuts. They might also have raised a monument to the small black man who made peanuts worth growing.

But Dr. Carver was already becoming famous around the country and the world for his scientific abilities. In 1923, he received the Springarn Medal for "highest achievement by a man or woman of African descent," and other medals and honors recognized his contributions.

In a day before the synthetic materials taken for granted today were known, Carver helped to create a new science called chemurgy. Chemurgy is a branch of chemistry dealing with the use of organic products, especially farm products, to manufacture new, non-food items.

Not all the products Carver developed are still being made commercially, and many never were. But Carver's most important "discovery" was the idea that renewable resources can serve as the raw materials of industry. George Washington Carver's answer to "The Great Peanut Puzzle" led to a new branch of science that is becoming more important than ever before, today and for the future.

5 The Clue in the Dying Dogs

People were dying, and George Minot could do nothing for them. In the early 1920s, patients who came into his Massachusetts office tired and weak, with faintly yellow skin, a slick, shiny tongue, and a numbness in their fingers and toes gave him a helpless feeling. He knew they were going to die.

George Richards Minot was interested in diseases of the blood. Pernicious anemia was one of the most mysterious and deadly of all those he studied. A victim's blood seemed to get thinner and thinner, as the life-giving red cells disappeared. Most doctors thought a poison had slipped into the blood, somehow, killing the red cells.

But Minot had a different idea. It is normal for red blood cells to die, he knew, because healthy blood is always renewing itself. The bone marrow makes enough new red cells to keep the blood in balance. In his dying patients, for some reason, that wasn't happening. Maybe the blood "forgot" how to grow new cells.

Minot drew tubes of blood from all his patients and smeared

the red droplets onto glass slides. He stained the cells with a brilliant blue dye, so he could see them better under his microscope.

What he saw was not really a surprise. Hardly any new cells were being produced. And those that were looked strange and immature. Something was very wrong, but Minot didn't know what.

Then Dr. Minot, himself, began to feel tired and weak. Always a thin man, he lost weight rapidly. His constant thirst drove him almost crazy, and he had to force himself to keep working when he felt too dizzy to stand up.

Being ill was nothing new. George had been sick most of his childhood. No one in his family expected the puny, skinny boy to live long enough to grow up.

But George fooled them. His health and strength both improved during his teens, and George managed to graduate high in his class at Harvard Medical School. Now, all that health and strength deserted him, again.

Minot was a doctor. He recognized the deadly symptoms. Before the other doctors told him, Minot guessed that he had diabetes, a disease every bit as fatal as pernicious anemia.

At the time, the only treatment for diabetes was a near-starvation diet. Diabetes is a digestive disease. It can be slowed if the patient eats only as much food as his body absolutely needs to stay alive.

Minot starved himself, but it didn't seem to help. He knew he was dying.

Then a medical miracle happened. Just in time, researchers in Canada discovered insulin, the missing hormone (body chemical) a diabetic's body needs. George Minot was one of the

George Richards Minot

first diabetics in the world to receive it.

With daily injections of insulin, Minot recovered quickly. He felt full of life and more determined than ever to save lives the way his had been saved.

Besides, Minot's own illness gave him a major clue to the mystery. Maybe pernicious anemia sufferers lacked something, too, the way diabetics lack insulin. Maybe he could find that something in food.

Minot quizzed his patients about every bite they ate. His zeal annoyed some of them. Even the other doctors thought he was overdoing it. Who cared exactly what each patient ate in a day?

George Minot did. He noticed right away that some of his patients were rather picky eaters, so he wrote out carefully balanced diets for them to follow. They did, but it didn't help.

Maybe a normally balanced diet was not enough. Maybe he was overlooking something. Minot began studying every book and paper he could find about the effects of different foods on the body. One of those papers described George Whipple's experiments on anemic dogs.

Dr. George Hoyt Whipple, pathologist, had just returned from a seven-year stay at the University of California to become head of the medical school at Rochester, New York. With him, he brought his collection of dying dogs.

Whipple wanted to learn how blood grows in the body and what foods and chemicals help it most. To do that, he carefully bled a group of dogs and then studied how their blood renewed itself. He kept the same dogs on the verge of dying for years, removing new blood as it formed with a syringe, so he could measure what factors helped it regrow fastest.

The faraway winner was liver. When Whipple fed liver to his dying dogs, their blood made new cells at a rapid rate. And the treatment caused tails to wag. Liver is one of a dog's favorite foods.

Minot read Whipple's paper in a scientific journal and almost put it away. He had already tried a high meat diet for some of his patients with no success, Anyway, blood-loss anemia, such as Whipple's dogs had, is nothing like pernicious anemia, where new blood simply doesn't form. But the figures in the paper were convincing. Liver really did produce new blood faster than any other food. Minot decided to give it a try.

He picked one of his healthier patients and suggested that the man eat liver twice a week. This patient was willing to try anything. Following Minot's orders, he began eating liver regularly. Almost at once, he began to feel a little better. And the stronger he felt, the more liver he ate, improving his condition even more.

Minot was pleased to see the man's dramatic improvement, but he couldn't help being a little skeptical. Pernicious anemia patients often perked up—temporarily. It might be just a coincidence. He decided to try the liver diet on one more patient.

This time, the doctor picked a woman who was near death. Almost too sick to swallow, she promised to try eating mashed liver twice a week.

Minot had other research projects under way, and an office full of patients. He forgot about the two liver-diet experiments until the man and woman walked into his office looking healthier than he had ever seen them. Their blood swarmed with normal red cells. It was almost a miracle.

Minot felt certain the miracle couldn't last. How could such a deadly disease be halted so easily? But any progress was some progress, even if it only helped for a short time. Minot called in other patients, to expand the experiment.

Soon George Minot had ten patients on liver. He watched them carefully, but the improvement did not slip away, as he expected. Instead, after more than a year, every patient on the "miracle" diet was feeling great. Normally, almost all of them would have been dead.

All that year, Minot kept the strange treatment quiet. He was afraid other doctors would laugh at him.

Finally, he let his friend, Dr. William Parry Murphy, in on the secret. Murphy was astounded. Ten patients with a fatal disease, all alive and well? This was too important to keep quiet any longer.

Together, the two doctors worked out the most effective treatment—half a pound of raw liver every day. That seemed to bring the quickest, most complete relief. Then they prescribed it to every pernicious anemia patient they could locate. They sometimes had to scrape the raw meat with a spoon to find a mouthful soft enough for patients too weak to chew.

At first, some of the sufferers gagged on the slimy red meat. It wasn't as popular with people as it was with Whipple's dogs. Minot could sympathize. He hated the taste of liver. But Murphy patiently encouraged them. Personally, the younger doctor thought liver tasted delicious, although he liked it better cooked.

No patient objected to the diet for more than a few days. Murphy called it a "thrill" to watch the peevish, dying victims suddenly start improving. Their symptoms went away, and they began to feel "an almost unbelievable sense of well-being," he said, as their blood came back to normal. It was worth eating raw liver, to feel so good again!

Other doctors did laugh, when they heard about the strange treatment. It sounded more like an "old wives' tale" than modern medicine. But they couldn't keep laughing at success. By 1926, Minot and Murphy had forty-five "dying" patients on the liver diet, all alive and well.

The "cure" was so simple anyone could try it. And since liver was inexpensive, almost everyone could afford it. Pernicious anemia soon changed from a hopeless disease to one that is easily managed.

The mystery was not over, because no one yet knew what caused pernicious anemia or how liver controlled it. The problem was far more complex than George Minot could have imagined, and it is not completely solved today. Researchers spent the next twenty years working on the case. They produced liver extracts (Minot helped on this part), liver injections, and, finally, tiny red crystals of a substance named vitamin B_{12}. The crystals could control the deadly disease far more easily than pounds of raw liver, and researchers began finding B_{12} in sources from oysters to antibiotic by-products to raw sewage.

But to Minot, the important thing was saving lives. Thanks to Whipple, Murphy, and Minot, no patient ever again had to die of pernicious anemia, and the three doctors received the 1934 Nobel Prize in Medicine and Physiology for their discovery.

As for the tiny red crystals, they started a new mystery. "The Clue in the Computer" in Chapter 10 tells their story.

6 The Riddle of the Returning Radiation

A fictional detective hardly ever solves a crime on the first try. Sometimes a second mystery develops. And a third. In fact, the detective may look like a bumbling idiot, halfway through the story, but he (or she) always has the last laugh.

Aluminum is the most common metal on earth. People use it in millions of ways. But one day in 1934, a pair of French scientists were amazed to discover invisible streams of radioactivity spewing from a tiny sheet of aluminum foil in their laboratory.

Aluminum is not radioactive. Where were the strange rays coming from? And why? Frédéric and Irene Joliot-Curie were determined to find out.

Radioactivity was like a giant jigsaw puzzle at the start of the twentieth century. Mysterious rays seemed to pour endlessly out of certain substances, and no one really understood how or why. For thirty years, scientists all over the world searched their labs and their brains for new "pieces" of information.

Irene Curie grew up with that search. In fact, her mother

coined the word "radioactivity." Irene was just a small child when her parents, Pierre and Marie Curie, received the 1903 Nobel Prize in Physics for discovering radium, the most radioactive element known. Pierre Curie died in 1906, but when Irene was a teenager, she saw her mother awarded a second Nobel Prize for more work with radioactivity.

At twenty-one, Irene became an official assistant at the Radium Institute her mother headed in Paris. Fascinated by radiation, she never stopped working on the "giant jigsaw puzzle" except to take enough time out to earn her doctor's degree in physics.

Frédéric Joliot came from a family of historians, but it was science that captured his interest. When Fred was six, he cut out a magazine picture of the famous Curies to hang on his wall. And, according to his mother, he "destroyed the bathroom" regularly, doing chemical experiments.

Fred's scientific training needed improvement when Marie Curie first hired him as a lab boy at the Institute, but he studied as he worked. And he walked, skied, swam, and fell in love with Marie's daughter, Irene.

Two years later, in 1926, Fred and Irene married. They joined their last names with a hyphen, so that the famous Curie name would not be lost. The two brilliant, hardworking physicists should have been ready to tackle any scientific mystery. But solving mysteries often takes a little luck, as well as skill. And at first, their luck was miserable.

In those days, the best way to study radioactivity was to bring something radioactive close to something that was not and see what happened. To the naked eye, mostly nothing happened. Radioactive rays are invisible.

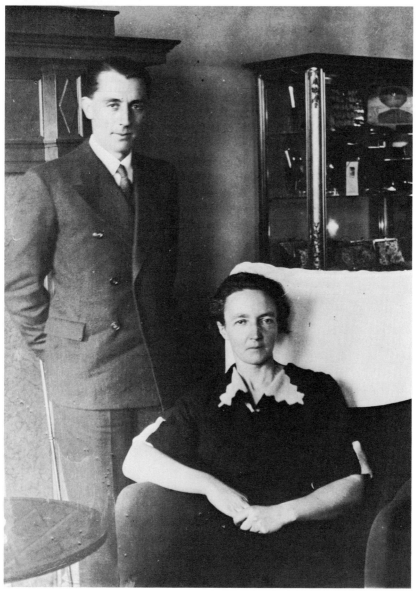

Wide World Photos

Frédéric and Irene Joliot-Curie

But scientists discovered ways to force the unseen rays to show themselves. To researchers, it was something like putting clothes on the invisible man.

Most rays turned out to be streams of particles, in small, medium, and large sizes (all far too tiny to see). By 1930, scientists knew about:

ELECTRONS—Small and fast. Electrons each have one charge of negative electricity, and they are usually found moving around outside the nucleus (center) of all atoms.

PROTONS—Medium-sized particles, almost two thousand times heavier than electrons. Protons each have one charge of positive electricity, and they are found inside the nucleus of every atom.

ALPHA RAYS—Beams of large particles, almost eight thousand times more massive than electrons. Alpha particles each have two units of positive electricity. French scientists call them "helions," but, in 1930, no one knew exactly what they were.

GAMMA RAYS—Tiny and superfast. Gamma rays are wavelike particles with no mass (or weight) that can be measured. They are like beams of pure energy.

Locating these tiny particles was not easy. As soon as Fred heard about any new device that could detect radioactive particles, he built it, and he and Irene put it to use in their basement lab. They soon became experts.

Fred's favorite device was the cloud chamber, which trapped moist, foggy air inside a glass case. If radioactivity moved through a cloud chamber, the particles left trails of bubbles in the mist.

Cloud chamber tracks last for less than a second, but a fast-moving researcher could take pictures of them. Electrons leave thin, beaded tracks. Proton trails are thicker, and helions draw wide stripes. Since magnets on the outside make the charged particle tracks bend to one side or the other, it is fairly simple to recognize the different kinds of particles as they streak their way across the cloud chamber's hazy interior.

Fred Joliot-Curie thought watching particle trails form in the mist was the most beautiful experience in life. Irene thought having a baby was more beautiful. Cloud chamber-watching came a close second.

Meanwhile, scientists kept finding hints that there might be other kinds of radiation. In 1931, the Joliot-Curies read about two German scientists who aimed a stream of helions at a light metal called beryllium. The beryllium shot back a spray of powerful radiation which could pass through a wall of lead fifteen centimeters thick! The Germans didn't know what the strange new radiation could be.

Fred and Irene wanted to find out. As a source of helions, they used a plate covered with pure, powdered polonium (another radioactive element discovered by Irene's mother), because it gave off a steady stream of alpha particles, or helions. And as the particles struck beryllium, rays of the unknown radiation began to bounce back.

The rays were powerful, knocking particles out of any atom they touched. Fred and Irene could see the telltale tracks beginning deep inside their cloud chamber. But the mysterious rays, themselves, left no track at all.

The Joliot-Curies decided the new rays must be some especially energetic gamma rays. They went to work, trying to prove it.

In England, another scientist read about Fred and Irene's efforts. He had a better guess about the mysterious radiation.

In 1932, James Chadwick identified the powerful ray as a stream of new particles about the same size as protons, but with no electrical charge. He named them neutrons. The credit (and the Nobel Prize) for solving the mystery was his.

News of Chadwick's discovery stunned Fred and Irene. They had been so close, but they had guessed wrong. Chadwick had solved their mystery! Disappointed, they went right to work studying the neutron, to see what could be learned about it. And almost at once, they found themselves staring at another mystery.

Neutrons leave no track when they pass through a cloud chamber, because they have no charge. But as they knock electrons out of other atoms, the electrons leave trails. The thin tracks start deep inside the mist and curve gently to the right.

Almost always, that is. Sometimes, when the Joliot-Curies shot neutrons through a chamber, they found thin tracks curving the wrong way.

Protons curve to the left in a magnetic field. But their tracks are much thicker. Helions also curve left, but they go through like a bulldozer, compared to the elfin tracks drawn by electrons.

So the new tracks did not seem to make sense. It was another mystery. Fred and Irene wrote a paper on what they found, but they couldn't explain it.

That same spring, 1932, the Joliot-Curies took a working vacation to the Swiss Alps. In a small laboratory which "hangs from the side of a mountain," as Fred wrote to his mother, they investigated cosmic rays.

Cosmic rays are radioactivity which falls on earth from outer space, and the French pair wanted to search them for neutrons. They chose the Alps to be close to the sky, where nothing else could interfere. And almost every day, they could ski on the high, snowy glaciers.

The trip was a failure, in one way. They found almost no neutrons. But as they examined their cloud chamber photographs closely, looking for the hard-to-spot neutrons, they noticed a few of the same tracks they had seen back in Paris. Thin, beaded tracks looked exactly like the tracks made by electrons, but they curved the wrong way. It was still a mystery, and they still had no answer.

That summer, an American physicist named Carl Anderson noticed the same unusual tracks. He had spent the summer mapping the trails of various particles through a special cloud chamber with a lead wall in the middle. He was familiar with every kind of track and trail drawn by all the known particles. These were something different.

But Anderson had an answer—the obvious answer. It had to be, he said, a new particle never noted before. It had to be a positive electron. He called his discovery a "positron."

Anderson proved his reasoning with some very careful experiments. It wasn't easy, because the new particle seemed to be quite rare. It only existed for a very short time before it met a normal electron and the two destroyed each other. But some physicists had already predicted that positive electrons might occur, and Anderson had the proof right on his photographic plates. (So did the Joliot-Curies, but they didn't realize it in time.) The world was convinced, and Anderson got a Nobel Prize for his discovery. The mystery was solved, and the Joliot-Curies had missed again.

Anderson's discovery came as a shock, but Fred and Irene swallowed their disappointment and kept on working. Finally, about a year later, they stumbled onto one more mystery.

The two scientists began bombarding aluminum with alpha rays from polonium, as they had done many times before. As the heavy helions crashed into atoms of aluminum, protons and neutrons began flying out. But when Fred and Irene carefully studied the pictures from their cloud chamber, they noticed something they had never noticed before. Surprisingly, positrons were flying out, too. They seemed to be getting one positron for every neutron.

Positrons are supposed to be rare. How could so many of them be radiating from an ordinary piece of metal?

The Joliot-Curies described the strange occurrence to other scientists at an international meeting in Brussels. Almost no one believed them. After all, measuring radiation is difficult and confusing. It was likely, the other scientists felt, that Fred and Irene were making some kind of mistake. Irene was so offended she almost left the meeting.

The two returned to Paris, determined to defend their results. To do that, they would have to find out what mysterious change was going on inside the aluminum. They would have to solve this mystery themselves!

Fred built a new cloud chamber, especially designed to pick up positron tracks. They also began using a new device called a Geiger counter, which clicks whenever charged particles touch the thin wires inside.

Then the Joliot-Curies set up a fresh sample of aluminum and started to recheck everything they had done before. They got the same, unexplainable results. Protons, neutrons, and positrons all were let loose by the bombarding helions. It didn't seem to make sense.

One day, Fred decided to see what would happen if he decreased the bombardment. Would one positron still come out for every neutron? Since he couldn't control what the polonium radiated, he moved it farther away from the sheet of foil.

As the bombardment slowed, so did the flow of protons and neutrons. But the positrons poured out as freely as before. Fred could see their thin, misty tracks clearly through the glass of his cloud chamber.

He could barely believe his eyes. It was as if a pianist took his hands off the keyboard, but the music kept on playing. Radioactivity had always bounced back from the aluminum while rays from the polonium were hitting it. But now, the foil was radiating all on its own!

Irene was working in another room. Fred went to get her. They put the polonium away in its lead-lined case and held the Geiger counter next to the sheet of aluminum. The counter began crackling loudly. It didn't stop for half an hour.

Geiger counters were all handmade in those days, and not very reliable. Sometimes they picked up cosmic rays through the roof. Sometimes they picked up stray radiation from other parts of the room. Sometimes they simply went crazy. Fred called in an assistant who was an expert with Geiger counters and asked him to check the device thoroughly.

Then Fred and Irene went home. They had an invitation to an important dinner and they couldn't avoid going. Besides, they wanted to give the lab assistant plenty of time to look over the counter. And the night gave them extra hours to think about the deepening mystery inside the aluminum atoms.

Scientists now knew, since the discovery of the neutron, that helions (alpha particles) are made of two protons and two neutrons. Chemists write it this way: $^4_2$He. The subscript, 2, stands for the number of protons (or units of positive charge). The superscript, 4, stands for the total number of neutrons and protons. Simple subtraction, $4 - 2 = 2$, tells the number of neutrons.

Irene went over all the possibilities in her head as she dressed for dinner. An atom of aluminum has thirteen protons and fourteen neutrons, written $^{27}_{13}$Al. The number of protons in an atom determines what kind of atom it is. If that number changes, the atom transmutes, or turns into a different kind of atom.

When an aluminum atom gets hit hard by a helion bullet, it can't quite absorb the whole thing. So, sometimes, it throws off one of the new protons. But because it has "swallowed" the rest of the helion—one proton and two neutrons—it becomes a fourteen-proton atom called silicon. Chemists write the change this way: One aluminum atom plus one helion changes to one silicon atom plus one proton.

$$^{27}_{13}\text{Al} \ + \ ^4_2\text{He} \ \rightarrow \ ^{30}_{14}\text{Si} \ + \ ^1_1\text{p}$$

Irene was sure this was one of the results they were getting. It accounted for the spray of protons they saw every time they bombarded aluminum.

But it didn't account for the neutrons or the positrons. Something else must be happening. Suppose, instead of throwing off a proton, some atoms of aluminum threw off a neutron. That would give:

$$^{27}_{13}\text{Al} \ + \ ^4_2\text{He} \ \rightarrow \ ^{30}_{15}\text{P} \ + \ ^1_0\text{n}$$

The new atom would now have fifteen protons. An atom with fifteen protons is a powdery, smelly element called phosphorus. Phosphorus is common, but in nature it always has sixteen neutrons, $^{31}_{15}P$. No other kind of phosphorus exists.

So with only fifteen neutrons, the "new" phosphorus atom Irene was speculating about would be unstable. In fact, if there were such a phosphorus atom, it ought to be radioactive.

That theory exactly fit the facts. The "new product" they had made by bombarding aluminum *was* radioactive. The two felt a thrill of excitement. "I wonder if we have not discovered artificial radioactivity?" Fred said to Irene.

The trick would be to find the radioactive phosphorus. Without it, they would have no proof. But the small square of aluminum would have only a few atoms of phosphorus. How could they capture them?

The Joliot-Curies got to the lab early, ready to recheck everything they had done. The Geiger counter was functioning perfectly. The assistant had left them a note guaranteeing it. And it told the same story as it had the day before. The mysterious radiation was definitely a stream of positrons, they concluded, and it definitely continued for half an hour after the polonium was removed.

But after three minutes, the radiation was only half as strong. And after another three minutes, half of what was left was gone.

Gradual decreasing by halves is normal for radioactive materials, they knew. The amount of time it takes for half the radiation to disappear is called the "half-life" of the material. Irene judged that the half-life of their radioactive phosphorus—if it were there at all—was about three minutes.

So if they wanted to prove that the mysterious radiating

substance was really phosphorus, they had about six minutes to find it. After that, most of it would have disappeared.

The Joliot-Curies were physicists, not chemists. They asked a chemist friend they happened to meet on the street how he would separate phosphorus from aluminum in three to six minutes. He threw up his hands in horror. No chemist worked that fast.

But Fred Joliot-Curie did. While Irene prepared a new sheet of radioactive aluminum foil, he set up the equipment for some fast chemical testing.

When the sample was ready, he dropped it into a glass container of hydrochloric acid. The metal began to bubble and froth. As it dissolved, Fred caught the escaping bubbles of gas in a thin-walled glass tube. Aluminum and silicon, he knew, would stay in the liquid solution. But any phosphorus would steam up into the tube.

The amount of phosphorus they collected would be too small to detect with any chemical test. But the radiation would give it away.

When the frothing stopped, the two carefully separated the glass containers. They held a Geiger counter next to the flask of hot liquid. Nothing happened.

Then they moved the counter close to the tube of gas. A steady clicking began. All the mysterious radiation had bubbled up into the glass. They had found their phosphorus. Fred was so excited he ran and jumped all around the room.

As the radioactive phosphorus broke down, they reasoned, it had to change one neutron into a proton. That would make it stable, again. To do that, it had to throw away one unit of positive charge, but almost no mass, or weight. And the only possible particle with a positive charge but almost no mass is a positron—exactly what they were finding.

The final equation, when they wrote it down, became: One radioactive phosphorus atom changes to one silicon atom plus one positron.

$$^{30}_{15}P \rightarrow \ ^{30}_{14}Si \ + \ ^{0}_{1}e^+ \ (e^+ \ = \ positron)$$

They announced their discovery on January 15, 1934. "With the neutron, we were too late. With the positron, we were too late," Fred told another scientist. "Now, we are in time."

It was especially satisfying to learn that a group of American researchers, this time, just missed making the discovery. Physicists in Berkeley, California, had been doing similar experiments, using much more elaborate equipment than Fred and Irene's handmade gear. Their source of helions was electric, and its "on-off" switch had been wired to the "on-off" switch of their Geiger counter. Turning both off at the same time, they had no way to discover that some of the radiation kept on coming after the bombardment stopped. (They never used Fred's favorite, the cloud chamber.)

When the Americans separated the wires, they saw what Fred and Irene had already reported. "We felt like kicking each other," one scientist said later.

Fred and Irene Joliot-Curie received the 1935 Nobel Prize in Chemistry (even though they were physicists) for the discovery of artificial radioactivity. By the day they accepted the award, dozens of other artificially radioactive substances had been produced in laboratories around the world. Today, there are thousands. And they have millions of uses, from medicine to nuclear research. The two French scientists opened a wide new door in the study and use of radioactivity, they solved a large section in the continuing "puzzle" of radiation, and they made Irene's mother, Marie Curie, very proud.

7 The Mystery of the
Missing Uranium, Case 1

In a classic "locked room" mystery, the crime is "impossible." The victim goes into his study and locks the door. A shot rings out. Police break in, to find only a bloodstain on the desk. The body has mysteriously vanished, and the detective must figure out who did what, and how.

In "The Mystery of the Missing Uranium," some uranium atoms are "shot" by a special gun. They disappear, leaving behind a confusing collection of chemicals. No one can figure out what happened, or what the mysterious chemicals are, because the right answer is "impossible."

Enrico Fermi thought he knew, but he was mostly wrong.

Ida Noddack had a suggestion, but her idea was labeled "ridiculous."

Irene Joliot-Curie said someone was making a mistake. Otto Hahn thought the same thing about her.

And Hahn, the "detective" on the case, kept trying to prove the wrong thing. Scientists all over Europe were caught in the middle of the biggest "locked room" mystery of the twentieth century and, at first, they didn't even know it.

The mystery opened in Italy. As soon as the Joliot-Curies discovered artificial radioactivity (see "The Riddle of the Returning Radiation," Chapter 6), scientists began racing to see who could produce the most interesting new radioactive atoms. And, like the Joliot-Curies' aluminum-which-turned-into-phosphorus, most of the new atoms were more massive (heavier) than the ones they started from. They acquired one or two extra protons in their nuclei.

Enrico Fermi, a young Italian physicist, led the race. Fermi had tried bombarding almost every known element with slow neutrons from his own invention called a "neutron gun," to see what would happen. The "gun" was a source of slow-moving neutrons which could be aimed at a target.

What happened most often, Fermi discovered, was that some of the neutron "bullets"—once they got inside an atom's nucleus—turned themselves into protons. Fermi could almost see this happening, because the change caused nuclei to act in a special, easily measured way. And since he already knew what the newly created, heavier atoms were likely to be, it was simple to identify them.

But uranium was not so simple. With 92 protons, uranium is already the most massive (heaviest) atom found in nature. Where could it go from there?

To find out, Fermi fired neutron "bullets" at a sample of pure uranium. It disappeared completely, leaving behind a mysterious mixture of elements.

But Fermi didn't see the mystery, because he was so sure he knew what had happened. He thought that most of the uranium atoms would add an extra proton, the way other elements did.

So the product, he assumed, consisted mostly of element #93. Element #93 would be a totally new atom, not seen on earth for millions of years, if ever.

And it looked as if he were right. Since element #93 does not exist in nature, no one knew how it should behave. It ought to be strongly radioactive, and the mixture was strongly radioactive. It would fit under element #75, rhenium, on the periodic chart of the elements, so it might act something like rhenium, chemically. Fermi thought he found something that did. So he called his discovery "eka-rhenium," element #93, using the traditional way to name suspected new elements.

But there were too few atoms to really test, they decayed too quickly, and the whole mess was too confusing. Fermi couldn't prove his theory.

Other scientists jumped into similar experiments, trying to be the first to find the proof. Almost no one doubted that Fermi had created a new element. After all, what else could it be?

The first clue came from Germany. Dr. Ida Tacke Noddack had helped discover rhenium while she was still a teenager, and she was suspicious of "eka-rhenium." No one can be sure of discovering a new element, she wrote in a magazine, until every other element has been checked out and eliminated. She suggested that uranium might "break into pieces" instead of getting bigger.

No one took Ida Noddack's clue seriously. It sounded as if she didn't understand atoms at all. "Everyone knew" it was impossible for atoms to break apart.

At this point, the "detective" entered the mystery. Otto Hahn and his research partner Lise Meitner were personal friends of Dr. Noddack, but they thought her strange idea was too embarrassing to mention. Hahn simply ignored it, he told her husband, because he "didn't want to make her look ridiculous."

A former co-worker of Hahn's, Aristide von Grosse, had a different theory. Fermi's "element #93," he thought, was really only ordinary element #91, protactinium. Von Grosse didn't think Fermi had checked carefully enough for atoms slightly smaller than uranium. Maybe it had lost a proton, instead of gaining one.

Hahn and Meitner had discovered protactinium together, and they knew more about it than any other research team. So they decided to see if von Grosse was right.

Otto Hahn was a chemist. He started his career as a teenager, doing experiments in the laundry room, and he had so much fun he switched from studying architecture into chemistry. Otto learned about radioactivity working with chemists in England and Canada. But when he came back to Germany, the University of Berlin did not offer radiochemistry in its curriculum. The chemistry department stuck him in an old, abandoned woodshop in the basement, to keep his strange-looking equipment out of sight.

Lise Meitner had even more trouble finding a place to work. She began studying physics at age twenty-two, after reading about the famous woman chemist, Marie Curie. An Austrian, Lise came to Germany in 1907, to finish her education. The University would not allow a female to set foot in the student laboratories, so she ended up in the same basement woodshop. She and Otto formed a partnership that lasted thirty-one years.

Some early discoveries, such as finding protactinium, made their names well known. But many of their admirers thought Lise was a man. One publisher tried to hire "Herr Doctor Lise

Meitner," whose "clear and accurate articles" he had admired in scientific magazines, to write for his encyclopedia. When he discovered she was "Fraulein Doctor Meitner," he withdrew the offer. "No woman," he declared, "would be capable of writing for [his] publication!" And while Otto Hahn soon became a full professor, Lise spent years as an unpaid assistant.

By the time the mystery began, it was 1935. Conditions had improved, and Lise was head of the radiophysics department. Otto headed the radiochemistry labs, and their work had expanded to fill parts of two large buildings.

When the team repeated Fermi's experiments, they found the same vanishing uranium and the same confusing mixture of chemicals. Hahn poured hydrogen sulfide into the brew, sending its rotten egg smell through the whole laboratory. Hydrogen sulfide precipitated the dissolved chemicals, turning them into solids, which could be studied more easily. Lise began measuring the radiation escaping from the mixture.

Together, they found four main substances. One disappeared after ten seconds and one after forty, but another two products had half-lives of thirteen and ninety minutes. The two scientists tried different chemical equations that might account for the changes taking place inside the unidentified atoms. It was the most confusing mess they had ever tackled.

Hahn and Meitner spent the next four years isolating more than a dozen decay products that appeared as the original mixture put out radiation, and they fit them all onto a complicated chart. There was absolutely no protactinium to be found, so von Grosse had to be wrong. They decided Fermi must be right about element #93. In fact, their chart listed possible new elements all the way up to element #96.

Otto Hahn and Lise Meitner

The overall scheme they worked out was elaborate and confusing, but it seemed to answer all the questions and solve Fermi's mystery. In fact, Otto Hahn began to think there was no real mystery at all. Uranium behaved just the same as every other element.

So the story moved to France. When Irene Joliot-Curie inspected Hahn and Meitner's elaborate chart, she immediately became suspicious. Why should it be so complicated? Why were there so many products? Something must be wrong, somewhere.

Irene and Pavel Savitch, a young assistant from Yugoslavia, aimed their own neutron gun at uranium. As usual, the uranium vanished. And right away, in the leftover radioactive "soup," they found more mystery.

When a neutron changes into a proton, it "throws away" a charge of negative electricity. A "new-born" electron shoots out of the nucleus with tremendous force, carrying that charge away. Rays of these powerful particles are called beta rays.

To simplify the mess left by the disappearing uranium, Joliot-Curie decided to pick out the one product with the most penetrating beta rays. She and Savitch covered the mixture with a thin sheet of copper. They found only one substance with beta radiation powerful enough to pass through the copper. It had a half-life of three and a half hours—a product Hahn and Meitner had never mentioned. It looked as if the German team had missed something important.

But Irene didn't know what the substance was. She thought she had located a new kind of thorium, element #90, and she published a paper explaining her view.

Otto Hahn read Irene Joliot-Curie's paper with annoyance.

First, there was no place on his chart for more thorium. Second, he was sure he had not missed any important substances. He and Lise wrote a letter to Irene, suggesting that *she* had made the error, not they. They suggested, politely, that if she would publish a retraction of her paper, they would not expose her mistake.

Now Irene was angry. She and Savitch redid everything, working with extra caution. The mysterious new substance still shot streams of beta rays right through copper.

But Hahn was right about one thing, they discovered. Whatever the mysterious product was, it wasn't thorium. It seemed, Joliot-Curie noticed, to resemble a much lighter element called lanthanum.

But lanthanum isn't normally radioactive, and it isn't a near neighbor of uranium on the periodic chart of the elements. So lanthanum, element #57, "couldn't possibly" be in the brew.

The mystery was getting deeper. Irene was very sure of her results, but not so sure what they meant. She and Savitch discussed their problem with all the other scientists at the Radium Institute, as different groups met to talk around the entrance hall or in Marie Curie's frequent laboratory teas in the garden. But no one had an answer.

Then a new thought struck Irene. Right under lanthanum on the periodic chart is an element called actinium, #89. Lanthanum and actinium are very much alike, chemically, and #89 is a neighbor—although not very near—to uranium. Perhaps the new substance was actinium.

Joliot-Curie and Savitch published another paper. It was not quite the retraction Hahn had asked for. In fact, it was worse.

The mystery substance definitely exists, Joliot-Curie wrote, and it "seems to be actinium or some other substance very similar to actinium or lanthanum." If she were right, Hahn and Meitner were very wrong.

Otto Hahn talked with Frédéric Joliot-Curie at a conference in May, 1938, and they had a few friendly arguments about the mystery. At the same meeting, Irene and Lise Meitner had a less friendly discussion. Hahn and Meitner each stated firmly that they expected to prove Madame Joliot-Curie wrong.

Back in France, Irene dug out an old technique her mother, Marie Curie, had developed to separate the radioactive actinium from all other elements. If the mystery substance was actinium, the technique should prove it beyond Hahn's doubt.

There was only a tiny amount of the substance present in the mixture, so Irene added a scoop of lanthanum to the brew. It should, she knew, act as a "carrier," to pick up and carry along every atom of the chemically-similar actinium almost to the end of the experiment. Then, using Marie Curie's technique, Irene and Pavel Savitch could separate the two. Only actinium would be left.

The two physicists followed all the steps carefully. But something went wrong. In the final separation, all the mystery substance stayed with the added lanthanum. They could spot it by measuring its radioactivity. There was no actinium at all.

Irene Joliot-Curie was mystified. Now, she was back to where she had started. What could the strange substance be?

Back in Germany, Otto Hahn and Lise Meitner were having problems of their own. And they weren't all scientific.

Usually, scientists try to keep politics out of the laboratory. But Adolf Hitler was in control in Germany, and Nazi politics invaded everything. Police inspectors arrived regularly to insure that every lab displayed a picture of Hitler and a copy of his book, *Mein Kampf*. They checked to see what sort of work was under way. And most of all, they searched for scientists who were Jewish. All Jews had to be fired immediately!

Lise Meitner was Jewish. As an Austrian citizen she was safe, at first. But in 1938, Germany invaded Austria, and her safety evaporated. Not only could she be fired, she could be arrested. With Otto's help, Lise escaped across the border, disguised as a tourist.

Fritz Strassmann, who had been working with them both on the uranium mystery, took over her unfinished experiments. But Hahn and Strassmann missed Lise Meitner's insight and her expertise in physics. The mystery seemed more hopelessly confusing than ever.

Working on a new lead, Hahn bombarded a fresh sample of uranium for several hours, with slow-moving neutrons from his neutron gun. This time, he planned to search for something new. He was looking for an element called radium.

Radium, element #88, is four protons lighter than uranium. Hahn didn't expect his uranium atoms to lose four protons all at once when hit by a neutron, but he thought some of the larger, unstable atoms on his chart might decay into radioactive radium. In fact, he had worked out all the calculations to show just how the decay happened. Finding radium in the mix would prove his whole scheme was true.

Only a very few radium atoms ought to exist, and they would be difficult to find. That, he supposed, must be why he had never noticed them before. So this time, he planned his new experiments with special care.

Hahn used the same "carrier" method Irene Joliot-Curie had

been trying, but he needed a different carrier. For radium, it would be an element called barium, #56, which sits right above radium on the periodic chart.

Hahn set up a series of experiments, adding barium and hydrochloric acid to every mixture. Beautiful white crystals began growing in every flask.

Most of the crystals were barium chloride, Hahn knew, from the carrier and the acid he had put in. But the crystals were slightly radioactive. That could only be, Hahn was certain, because a few crystals of radium chloride were trapped among the rest. Nothing else made sense.

Hahn felt sure he had proved his theory. "Hence, if we disregard the barium, itself," he wrote in a paper describing the results, "only radium is left."

Then the trouble started. When Hahn and Strassmann tried to separate the radium from the added barium, the separation didn't work. It almost seemed as if the "radium" in the mixture were actually barium. And that, Hahn knew, was "impossible."

Hahn and Strassmann considered ignoring the disappointing news. So what if they couldn't actually separate out the radium. They "knew" it was there.

Their research paper about "radium crystals" was almost ready to mail when Fritz Strassmann picked up a new magazine. He stared at another article by Joliot-Curie and Savitch.

Hahn was smoking a cigar when Strassmann handed him the article. Hahn refused to read it. He was tired, he said, of "our lady friend," and her "out-dated experiments."

Strassmann insisted. Finally, Hahn started to read. Then he put down his cigar, unfinished, and ran downstairs to the lab.

The article didn't really say much. It reported, essentially, that the French team had given up. The mystery substance they were chasing had proved to be so much like lanthanum there was no way but radioactivity to tell them apart.

Irene Joliot-Curie had no explanation. She simply stated the results as she found them. And once again, the Nobel Prize-winning physicist had missed solving a major mystery (see Chapter 6 "The Riddle of the Returning Radiation").

But her final paper provided the one clue Hahn needed. He had always supposed she was doing something wrong. But what if she were right! What if her unidentified substance *was* lanthanum. And suppose his own confusing reaction product *was* barium, not radium. That would mean he had been looking for the wrong thing all these years. That would mean the uranium had "burst" into smaller atoms.

Hahn and Strassmann repeated everything, looking at the results in a whole new way. While they had been looking for large atoms, small ones had been hiding under their noses. If they had not thought finding barium in the mixture was impossible, they would have noticed it weeks, months, years ago.

And lanthanum, too. When they tried the experiment in Irene's slightly different way, they found her mystery substance— unmistakably lanthanum. The "impossible" was impossible no longer.

But finding the chemicals was not enough. They had to be able to explain what was happening. That needed a physicist's approach.

Hahn and Strassmann were both chemists. They tried subtracting the atomic weight (total number of neutrons and protons) of barium from uranium and found several possibilities for what the rest of the atom might have become. None of them made much sense. Something was still a mystery.

Finally, they settled for adding a note to their paper on "radium salts." At the bottom, they wrote that it was likely all the salts described were actually barium, and that, somehow, "against all previous experience," the atom had "burst" into smaller fragments. "It is possible," they added cautiously, "that a number of rare accidents have fooled us into making erroneous observations."

Then they dropped the manuscript into the mail. Right away, Otto Hahn wished he could get it back. He was afraid everyone would laugh at the idea of "bursting atoms" the way he had laughed at Ida Noddack.

Hahn thought of Lise Meitner. Would she laugh, too? He badly needed her advice, so he sat down and wrote her a letter, describing the whole series of experiments. He dropped it in the mail, too, addressed to the university in Sweden, where she was now working.

For Christmas, 1938, Lise was on vacation at a Swedish sea-coast resort. When the letter arrived, she took it out into the sparkling snow to read in privacy.

The single page was more of a scientific report than a letter, and most of the experiments involved steps she remembered well. The startling part came at the end.

Lise Meitner didn't laugh. She respected Otto's abilities as a chemist. If he said the "radium" was really barium, then it must *be* barium. Now for the physics. How did the barium get there?

Meitner began to pace up and down, in snow over her shoe-tops. She remembered her friend Ida Noddack's strange idea. And she thought about drops of liquid and the way they can shatter under force, like raindrops hitting glass.

Suppose a nucleus acts the same way. Suppose a heavy atom, such as uranium, actually splits in two when hit by a neutron "bullet." What a fascinating idea!

Lise needed someone to talk to. Otto Hahn was hundreds of miles away, in enemy territory, but her nephew Otto Frisch was vacationing at a nearby hotel. And he was a physicist, too. Lise Meitner set off walking through the snow.

When she found Frisch, he was in no mood to talk. His mind was on an experiment of his own. Otto Frisch strapped on skis and slid out onto the snow, followed by his aunt, who was still plowing along in wet shoes. As they skiied and waded through the woods, Meitner explained Hahn's problem and her own theory.

"It took her a little while to make me listen," Frisch admitted later.

Finally, he began to pay attention. They sat down on a fallen log to work out the details.

Hahn's result and his idea had to be correct, they agreed. His only mistake was in trying to subtract atomic weight, the way a chemist would, instead of atomic number, the way a physicist would. (Atomic weight is the total number of protons and neutrons in a nucleus; atomic number is only the protons.)

Meitner knew all the elements and their numbers by heart. She didn't need a periodic chart to do the subtraction in her head. Uranium-92 minus barium-56 leaves krypton-36. And krypton is an invisible gas. There was no way Hahn could have found the missing half of the atom unless he knew exactly what to look for.

The "locked room" mystery was actually simple. Uranium had split into two smaller atoms. Some atoms had split into barium and krypton, and there were probably other pairs. No wonder the brew had seemed so complicated!

Otto Frisch cut short his vacation to race back to the laboratory. Once he knew what to look for, proving that the atom had split was easy. Frisch even coined a name for the process, fission, from the name biologists give to splitting cells.

Frisch worked under Niels Bohr, one of the most famous scientists of the day. When he described Hahn's experiments and Meitner's conclusions, Bohr struck himself in the forehead with his fist. "Oh, what idiots we have been," he said.

Otto Hahn won the 1944 Nobel Prize in Chemistry for the discovery of atomic fission. Why Lise Meitner wasn't included in the award is another mystery, but she and Fritz Strassmann and Hahn all shared the 1966 Enrico Fermi Award for their joint efforts.

The discovery came at a crucial time in history. World War II was just beginning, and atomic (now called nuclear) fission led directly to the first atomic bomb. It also led to advances in medicine, power production, and all levels of scientific knowledge. The mystery of the missing uranium opened the door on the Nuclear Age. It changed the world forever.

8 The Case of the Vanishing Virus

Summer was a time of fear. During the warm weather "polio season," parents of young children worried about almost everything. Would swimming in a public pool spread polio? Could you catch it at a country fair? Did strenuous games such as soccer and baseball make a child more susceptible? No one knew. Polio was a terrifying mystery disease.

In 1949, 43,000 people, mostly children, fell ill with poliomyelitis. More than two thousand victims died. Thousands more became paralyzed; their legs, sometimes even their breathing, were crippled by the relentless, nerve-destroying disease.

Yet it all started with simple symptoms—headache, slight fever, nausea. Any sign of summer illness was enough to send parents into a panic.

There was no mystery about the cause of polio. It was a virus, common in most parts of the world. In primitive times, babies usually caught it sometime during their first year of life. A few died, but most became immune. Their blood developed special antibodies that could fight off the polio virus whenever it attacked again.

But in modern times, cleanliness and sanitation protected babies from the powerful virus. They never got a chance to form a natural immunity. That meant that almost all modern children were vulnerable to polio if it happened their way. The deadly crippler could strike whenever it wanted, and the older the child it hit, the more serious the results could be.

There was no cure for polio, no protection, and no prevention. The sight of active children suddenly doomed to crutches or the dreaded "iron lung" breathing machine for the rest of their lives horrified everyone, but no one knew what to do. Polio was a major mystery of modern medicine.

That's why John Enders wanted nothing to do with polio. The mystery intrigued him, but he hated noise and commotion and publicity. If "everyone else" in the field of virology was working on the polio problem, urged on by parents, politicians, and even President Franklin Roosevelt (himself a polio victim), all wanting an answer right away, then Enders preferred to turn his talents in some other direction. After all, the world abounded with mysterious viruses needing study. Enders decided to work on mumps.

John Franklin Enders was a late-blooming scientist. Intending to become an English professor, he had almost earned a Ph.D. degree in literature when he moved into a boardinghouse filled with medical students. Their work sounded far more interesting than his, especially the research into the causes of disease. After one of his housemates introduced him to the famous Dr. Hans Zinser, of the bacteriology department at Harvard, John switched his field of study.

It meant starting graduate school all over, almost, but John had finally found what he wanted to do. He came from a wealthy family, so he could afford a few extra years of school. When

John Enders completed the last requirements for his Ph.D., it was in science instead of literature.

Viruses interested the newly graduated scientist most. They were too tiny to see by any microscopes readily available at that time, and researchers had to guess where they were by watching for the damage they did.

By the end of World War II, Enders was an accomplished virologist. He had developed a vaccine to save cats from deadly feline distemper. He was making progress on a vaccine for mumps. But he was still only an unknown assistant professor at Harvard Medical School.

Enders didn't mind being unknown. Impressive titles and higher salaries weren't important to him. What he wanted was more time to study viruses. He had to spend so many hours teaching bacteriology to medical students that he had very little time left for his real love—research.

Then his career got a giant boost. Nearby Children's Hospital asked Enders to establish a new research laboratory. They assigned him a small brick building and enough money to set up the kind of lab he had always wanted. He would be free to spend all his time looking for viruses. All he had to do was train doctors who wanted to be researchers, as his assistants. This was just the opportunity he had been waiting for.

John Enders knew exactly the sort of research he wanted to do. All his work on mumps so far had been complicated by monkeys. Every strain of mumps virus had to be grown inside live, active monkeys, because that was the only place it would thrive. Viruses only grow inside living cells, and some are very particular about what kind.

But monkeys are noisy, troublesome, and expensive. Even

eggs, where some viruses will grow, are a nuisance. Enders planned to find a way to raise hard-to-grow viruses inside cheap, quiet test tubes.

When Tom Weller arrived from his wartime assignment in Puerto Rico, not much was happening yet, inside the red brick building. He found Enders busy ordering and sorting new equipment.

Dr. Thomas Weller, M.D., had been studying tropical diseases for the Army during the war, but children were his favorite patients. He hoped to find a vaccine to prevent chicken pox.

Working together, Enders and Weller soon put the laboratory into operating shape. Each began planning the first series of experiments for his pet project—mumps for Enders and chicken pox for Weller. Then another assistant arrived.

Dr. Frederick Chapman Robbins, M.D., came from an Army post in Italy to the new Massachusetts laboratory. He preferred children to soldiers, too, and he was looking forward to working with Enders. The older man had a careful, controlled research style Robbins admired. But Robbins had one stipulation. He didn't want to work with polio.

That was quite all right with John Enders. Neither did he.

The problem with polio research was not merely the glaring publicity attached. It was the hopelessness of the whole thing. Researchers had been trying for years to find a way to make a vaccine to prevent polio, but wherever they tried to grow the deadly virus, it vanished.

The only place to grow the polio virus, it seemed, was not just inside monkeys, but inside the *brains and spines* of monkeys. Nerve tissue appeared to be the only place the crippling virus could thrive. That made sense, because nerve damage causes

John Franklin Enders and Thomas Huckle Weller

the horrible, paralyzing effect polio can have on its victims.

But nerve tissue cannot be used to make a vaccine, because it sets up an allergic reaction inside other animals or humans that could be even deadlier than polio. So the dilemma was clear: no polio virus without nerve tissue, and no vaccine *with* nerve tissue. No one could think of a way around the problem.

The last thing John Enders wanted was another virus that would only grow inside monkeys. He suggested that Robbins pick any other project he liked.

Fred Robbins decided to work on the cause of infant diarrhea, which often plagued newborn babies in hospital nurseries. He set up a series of experiments to try and outline the problem.

By April, 1947, all three men had their projects under way. As researchers-in-training, Weller and Robbins also assisted John Enders with his mumps problem. The two young doctors had been classmates at Harvard, and they worked well together. But they sometimes thought their department head was a little too cautious. He liked to take everything so slowly!

The team experimented with every kind of material that might possibly let viruses grow in a glass container, instead of a furry one or a fragile egg shell. Bacteria, they knew, will grow in almost any kind of nourishing "soup," but viruses only grow in living cells. The trick is to keep the right kind of cells alive in a test tube long enough for the viruses to grow.

Enders' group was not the first to try growing viruses in a glass flask, but fast-growing bacteria almost always spoiled the effort. Once bacteria took over, it was impossible to measure the effects of the virus. The only way to stop them was to "wash" the virus-growing cells with fresh fluid and move them to a clean flask every two or three days.

Some researchers had tried adding the new "wonder drug," penicillin, but bacteria still caused trouble. The scientists had to work fast, to stay ahead. Most of them eventually gave up in disgust.

John Enders didn't like working fast. He thought of a better idea. What if he added both penicillin and another, even newer "wonder drug" called streptomycin? He and Tom Enders set up a series of flasks with the two drugs and some ready-to-hatch chicken egg cells in a special broth of ox blood. Carefully, they added cells containing mumps virus to their "witches' brew" of ingredients.

For the first time, the flasks stayed completely free of bacteria. For the first time, the team didn't have to disturb the fragile cells by bathing them in clean broth so often. And, for the first time, the mumps virus began to flourish.

In a matter of days, all three men were using the two drugs in all their experiments. Since antibiotics have no effect on viruses, they didn't slow down virus multiplication at all. But they killed the invading bacteria completely, giving the tinier viruses a clear field.

Enders' mumps virus began growing so well in a flask that a few more months of work put the problem completely under control. It was now possible to grow mumps virus in a tissue culture in glass with ease. No more monkeys!

The two assistants turned back to their own experiments. Meanwhile John Enders, never in a hurry, began thinking about what needed doing next.

Weller's chicken pox virus turned out to be every bit as hard to grow as mumps—perhaps harder. It didn't like growing on most kinds of cells. So after months of trial and error, Weller decided to find it some human cells to attack.

Human cells are not easy to obtain, for laboratory use. Weller managed to get some human embryonic tissue, from the bodies of fetuses that died from miscarriage or premature birth.

Weller set up rows of glass flasks containing tiny bits of skin and muscle tissue from the embryos, plus the two drugs and a broth that would keep the cells alive. He injected almost half the flasks with strains of chicken pox virus. An equal number he kept as controls.

When he was done, there were several flasks left over. It would be a shame to let the rare and valuable human cells go to waste, so he looked around for something else to grow.

In John Enders' freezer was a carefully labelled vial containing a frozen mouse brain. Inside the cells of the brain, hidden from the eye, lay the virus Enders and Robbins had wanted to ignore. It probably won't grow anyway, Weller thought, but why not give polio a try?

Tom Weller cleared the idea, first, with Dr. Enders. Enders had never been able to get the polio mystery completely out of his mind. Besides, the new lab they were working in was partially funded by the National Polio Foundation. The situation seemed perfect, so Enders told Weller to go ahead.

Then Enders thought about it a little longer. As long as the polio virus was out of the freezer, why not try it someplace else? Enders took the vial over to Fred Robbins, who had just set up a row of fresh flasks, each containing bits of mouse intestine. Fred had been trying to grow the diarrhea virus, but had been having almost no luck.

"I've been wondering about polio virus growing in the intestine," Enders said. "Why don't you try it?"

Both young doctors inoculated flasks with the deadly virus and then set them back safely out of the way. There was nothing to do, then, but wait a week or so to see what would happen.

They didn't expect much. "Everyone knew" polio only grew on nerve tissue, at least in the laboratory.

Normally, polio researchers would have to wash down all the cells in the flasks every two or three days, to clean away the growing bacteria. But no bacteria were growing in Enders' double-antibiotic broth. They left the flasks undisturbed for ninety-six hours.

After four days, the three carefully drew off all the fluid they could suck into a glass pipette and replaced it with fresh. There was no need to move the cells to a clean flask.

The cells needed fresh broth to stay alive, but the men had another reason for drawing off the first fluid. If the virus was not multiplying, diluting it should reduce its strength. But if viruses were growing in the cells, then the brew might be far more potent than before. As yet, there was no way to tell.

After eight days, they injected fluid from every flask, including some of the virus-free controls, into laboratory mice. Then they waited, again.

Before long, some of the mice began dragging limp hind legs around the cages. Paralysis set in quickly. Others stopped breathing and died. The three researchers could hardly believe their eyes. Polio!

All of the paralyzed, dead, and dying mice had received injections from Weller's human embryo culture cells. Not a one was from a control or from Robbins' mouse intestine cultures. Those mice stayed as frisky as ever.

The trouble was, so did several of the mice which had been injected with Weller's polio virus. Apparently the crippling virus did not grow in all of Weller's flasks—only in one.

But that was more than any other researcher had been able to accomplish. They had shown that polio could be grown outside of nerve cells, hadn't they? Weller and Robbins felt a thrill of excitement.

Enders stayed calm. He was not so sure they had discovered anything at all. Maybe the mice died of something else. Maybe the original strain hadn't been diluted enough. Any of a hundred things could be wrong. He insisted they set up new flasks and start all over.

They did, but they also saved the fluids which had killed the mice. These, they rediluted, being careful not to disturb the cells. Every week or so, they tested more mice. Several of the flasks, diluted again and again, killed more mice than ever. The fluid could even kill monkeys. The deadly virus *had* to be multiplying!

After a few months, the three men had a system well organized. Polio virus was carefully placed on human embryo cells inside glass flasks partly filled with salt water, ox serum (blood with the red cells removed), the penicillin and streptomycin, plus some sixty other chemicals. The complex fluid made an ideal place to keep cells alive.

Every few days, the team diluted the liquid in the flasks. And every week, they injected more of it into mice and monkeys. Not even cautious John Enders could ignore the results. Mice and monkeys were dying of polio, right before their eyes. The virus that "couldn't be grown" in non-nerve tissue was growing in the cells of unborn babies.

Enders wanted absolute proof before he announced such a startling discovery to a polio-frantic public. He wished he had some way of seeing the tiny viruses directly. Then one of the men thought of the next best thing.

The team always put a drop or two of a dye called phenol red in each flask, to let them know the cells were still alive. Healthy cells produce acid, and acid turns the pinkish phenol red to an orange color and finally to yellow. The control flasks of every batch turned yellow every time, in just a few days. But in the flasks containing polio virus, this didn't happen as fast. The liquid stayed pink or light orange days longer, because the virus was injuring cells as it multiplied. Injured cells do not produce as much acid as healthy ones, so the color of fluid inside each flask gave a clue as to what was happening inside. They could tell if the virus was growing, without killing so many mice. It was just the kind of direct evidence Enders needed.

All other work in the lab stopped. Chicken pox, infantile diarrhea, and even mumps were forgotten. The team developed a faster method, using stoppered test tubes lying on their sides in a roller drum that could be rotated to "air" the cells.

By mid-1949, in flasks and tubes all around the room, Enders' team had polio growing on several kinds of human tissue. It even began to multiply in bits of monkey kidney. The researchers began to wonder what had been so difficult and mysterious about growing polio, all along.

But there was one thing they had almost forgotten. Using the two antibiotics to kill bacteria gave them the time to be slow and careful. Every researcher in the past had been rushing, trying to force the stubborn virus to grow before the bacteria took over. Neither the polio virus nor John Enders liked to be rushed.

For the final proof that what they were growing was really polio, Enders asked a colleague for some blood serum from a monkey which had recovered from the disease. He put several drops of the clear serum into a few of his virus-growing test tubes. Growth stopped. Polio antibodies from the monkey's blood killed the virus every time.

There was no longer any doubt. John Enders and his team had grown exactly what they thought they had—the dreaded virus of polio. And they had grown it in several kinds of non-nerve tissue, including laboratory monkey. There was nothing to stop scientists, now, from developing a vaccine. Polio could finally be conquered.

Enders wasn't interested in developing a vaccine. His lab was "not set up for" that kind of research, he said, and Weller and Robbins each had another job offer they wanted to take. So they let other researchers take over.

"Dr. John Enders pitched a long forward pass," Jonas Salk told *Current Biography* later, "and I happened to be in the right spot to receive it." In 1955, the Salk polio vaccine went on the market. The safer Sabin "sugar cube" vaccine replaced it a few years later. Polio quickly changed from a summer nightmare to a rare disease.

Enders, Weller, and Robbins shared the 1954 Nobel Prize

for Medicine. John Enders called the sharing "symbolic," because scientific discoveries are always based, he said, on "the work of many people." And the work is still going on, as researchers use Enders' technique to study other hard-to-grow viruses. His slow, cautious effort paid long-lasting dividends.

9 The Clue in the

Mummy's Tomb

In his television detective series, Lieutenant Colombo always solves the murder mentally in the first few minutes. He seeks out the most obvious suspect. The rest of the hour he spends trying to prove his solution.

In his chemical laboratory, Willard Frank Libby came across a clue to a mystery centuries old. Once he thought about it, the solution was obvious. But proving it took more than an hour.

For years, archaeologists played guessing games with the past. Sometimes they could date ancient objects and civilizations by studying their history. Sometimes they could trace dates by comparing the pottery or weapons in one place to those in another. Or by examining what village was built on top of another.

There are dozens of different ways. But often archaeologists simply had to make the best guess they could, based on knowledge and experience.

It was frustrating. If a farmer uncovered an old bone or the remains of an ancient campfire in his field, there was no dependable way to tell its age. If a pair of prehistoric sandals turned up in the dark depths of a cave, it was impossible to discover just when the wearer had abandoned them there.

Even worse, no one could be sure that the educated guesses archaeologists ventured were accurate. Did farming travel from Egypt to America, or did it start in both places at about the same time? Did metalworking skills spread from the Aegean to the Balkans, or was it the other way around? Dating the past was a worldwide mystery, with no solution in sight.

No ancient puzzle was bothering Dr. Willard Libby in 1946, as he set up operations at the Institute of Nuclear Studies, University of Chicago. This new position was his first chance to do chemical research on his own since the war had interrupted everything.

Tall, lanky Bill Libby had spent the five years of World War II enmeshed in secret government research on the atomic bomb. He couldn't even tell his wife the slightest thing about what he was doing. Now, he was glad to be free. He had an idea of his own he wanted to check out.

Radioactivity was Bill's first love. In graduate school he had invented a way to measure extra-small amounts of radiation. As a radiochemist, he had learned a great deal about the cosmic rays that crash into earth from outer space. Now, he wanted to combine the two skills. He planned to use his measuring technique to search for small, hard-to-detect radioactive effects that cosmic rays might have on nature.

Bill Libby knew where to start. Cosmic rays are too energetic to trace directly with any tools that were available in the '40s, but they do one thing that is easy to measure. The speedy rays knock neutrons out of passing atoms.

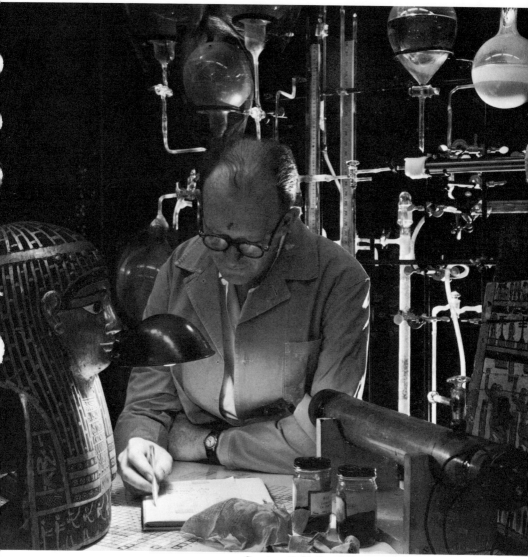

Willard Frank Libby by Volkmer Wentzel

But what do those neutrons do next, if anything? No one knew for sure.

They had a pretty good idea. At five or six miles above earth, the most common thing around is nitrogen. And neutron "bullets" ricocheting through the thin air might do a "magic act" when they bumped into atoms of nitrogen. They might change those atoms into atoms of carbon, like a magician's scarf "turns into" a bouquet of flowers.

Of course, Dr. Libby knew the trick behind the magic. Nitrogen always has seven protons. If a flying neutron knocks out one of those protons, the atom will have only six left. And an atom with six protons is carbon.

But, so what? Several scientists had already predicted the nitrogen-carbon transformation, but nitrogen and carbon are both common and harmless. Who would notice if some of them switched identities?

Bill Libby, that's who, because of one strange fact. Ordinary carbon has six protons and six neutrons in its nucleus. The newly made carbon would have two extra neutrons—one from the nitrogen and one from the cosmic ray bullet. And two extra neutrons should turn ordinary carbon into Bill's favorite kind of atom: radioactive.

Radioactive carbon? It sounded ridiculous. True, a few atoms of carbon-14 (6 protons plus 8 neutrons equals 14) had been formed in a laboratory, but no one had ever supposed such an unusual kind of atom existed in nature.

Except Bill Libby. He was sure it was there and determined to find it.

So how do you look for solitary carbon atoms floating high above earth? Obviously, Libby figured, you don't. You decide what they will do next. Carbon dioxide is the gas animals breathe out and plants take in, and it's a good bet that CO_2 is what lone, airborne atoms will turn into. But this CO_2 would be special. It would be radioactive. If so, no one had ever noticed it.

When you're looking for a needle in a world-sized haystack, it helps to know how big the needle is. According to pages and pages of calculations Libby and his students made, the radiocarbon "needle" would be quite small. They predicted one carbon-14 atom for every trillion atoms of carbon-12.

For a while, Libby and his crew were stumped. Where could they look for something that was one part in a million million? Then someone located a laboratory in Pennsylvania with equipment designed to concentrate another rare kind of carbon, carbon-13. Perhaps it would work for their project, too.

Bill Libby and a few students set out from Chicago to Pennsylvania. They had to find an answer fast, before their money ran out.

The equipment they borrowed had been set up to work on methane gas, the gas burned in stoves and furnaces. Methane is composed of carbon and hydrogen, CH_4. If Bill's theories proved right, some of that carbon should be carbon-14.

The team began to check. First, they thought of the methane gas that comes out of oil wells.

But natural gas from wells didn't work. Carbon-14 has a half-life (the way scientists measure how long radioactivity lasts) of 5,730 years. That means that in five thousand, seven hundred and thirty years, half the radioactive atoms underground would have decayed back to nitrogen. And another half in the next five thousand, and so on. Since the methane in oil wells is millions of years old, all the radiocarbon would be gone. Sure enough, it was.

Bill felt frustrated. All around him were trees and grass and insects that must have carbon-14 inside their bodies, and he had no way to prove it. The only equipment he could find worked only on methane.

Bill Libby's co-workers called him "Wild Bill," for his lively methods, and he lived up to his nickname. "Wild Bill" searched everywhere for a source of *new* methane gas and he found it, in the Baltimore sewers, not far from the lab where they were working.

Sewage gives off methane gas, formed from decomposing animal matter. It would be "fresh" methane—just the kind Bill needed.

The students collected samples of the smelly sewer air and separated out its methane. Carefully, they concentrated the samples for heavy carbon atoms, using the expensive, borrowed equipment. Testing the result with a Geiger counter, to measure radioactivity, brought a steady stream of clicking noises.

The team felt like cheering. The radiocarbon they were searching for definitely existed.

And now that they knew how to find it, "Wild Bill" and his crew began looking for other materials to test. They adapted the procedure to concentrate the carbon dioxide in ocean water and measured its radioactivity. The number of clicks matched in water samples from all parts of the world.

Then they ground up seashells. They burned and tested wood samples from Chicago to Palestine to Sweden. It began to look as if the amount of radiocarbon everywhere stayed at a constant level. For every new carbon-14 atom that cosmic rays created, another one decayed.

As long as plants took in carbon dioxide from the air, the amount of radiocarbon in plant matter had to stay the same. A new one in for every one decayed. And as long as animals ate plants (or ate other animals that ate plants), the amount of carbon-14 in their tissues stayed constant, too. For all living things, the ratio seemed to be one carbon-14 for every trillion carbon-12.

All this sounded interesting, but far more expensive than useful. Testing just the first few samples had pushed the team way over budget, and it seemed as if they ought to abandon the whole line of research.

But Willard Libby didn't want to give up, because along the way he had thought of an incredible idea. If living plants and animals take in and lose radiocarbon at a steady rate, what happens when they die?

After death, animals no longer breathe or eat. Plants no longer take in carbon dioxide from the air. In fact, dead things no longer absorb any new carbon-14 from anywhere. But the carbon-14 already inside their bodies keeps right on decaying.

If that is true, Bill reasoned, then matter from plants and animals long dead should have less radiocarbon in it than living creatures. And the longer ago they died, the less they should have.

Suddenly, Bill Libby could see the answer to the age-old mystery. It might be possible to date ancient objects which had once been alive by measuring the amount of carbon-14 they had left.

Bill Libby was not an archaeologist, but his background came close. As a college sophomore studying mining engineering, he accidentally met two graduate students outside his boarding-house one day. Their tales of chemical research excited Bill far more than mining did, and he switched his major to chemistry.

But in his head, the young scientist filed away all he had already learned about geology and the layers of the earth and about the way archaeologists use them to discover which ancient relics are older than which others. He also knew about the frustrating puzzles scientists have to solve, trying to date the past.

Using carbon-14 to help solve those puzzles made a fabulous theory. But would it work? And even if it did, would it be of any use when the test was so expensive it might cost hundreds of thousands of dollars just to date one mummy?

Libby and his students got busy. Using brass tubing at $51.70 per hundred pound, plus stainless steel, copper and copper-coated iron wire, they constructed a screen scintillation counter which could measure radioactive atoms without concentrating them. Using more metal tubing, glass, and wire, mixed with a lot of talent and ingenuity, they concocted a method for burn-ing everything but the carbon out of a sample and then spread-ing it in a thin layer. They needed about six grams of carbon to make the system work, but it was far cheaper than the old method.

The whole effort took several years. Finally, it paid off. When the team placed a properly treated new sample in front of the screen, the counter flashed a steady fifteen sparks per minute per gram of carbon.

Now they were ready to tackle the mystery. Dr. Libby wrote

to several different archaeologists, asking their help.

None of the archaeologists had ever heard of carbon-14, but they were willing to give the strange idea a try. They mailed him some samples they could spare, with dates which had been carefully worked out by some historical method.

The first item the crew tested was a chunk of acacia wood beam, from the pyramid of an ancient pharaoh. Djoser ruled Egypt about 4,900 years ago.

Unfortunately, the carbon-14 tests reported that the wood was centuries older. Something was wrong.

Libby tried again. With his students, he washed another sample in carbon-free chemicals to get rid of every trace of modern contamination. He used tweezers and a magnifying glass to remove every tiny bit of debris. He tinkered with the counters, adjusting them as accurately as he could.

This time, the result was closer. But it was not good enough. They kept trying.

By the eighty-first sample, the method was working dependably. The team burned and tested a tiny chunk of cypress wood from a funeral boat in the Chicago Natural History Museum. The boat had belonged to Pharaoh Sesostris III, who lived 3,750 years before.

Carbon-14 tests dated the wood chip at 3,621 years old, plus or minus 180 years. Answers that close easily satisfy a science used to dealing in thousands of years.

Then, just when he was feeling secure, Libby got a rude shock. A piece of coffin lid threw a wild number of flashes across the screen. The mummy inside the sarcophagus was more than two thousand years old, but the wooden lid tested almost new.

Libby's team rechecked everything and ran the test again. Same answer. Finally, Dr. Libby contacted the museum director. Would he please recheck, too? He did, and discovered that the sarcophagus lid was a modern-made fake.

But after three years of hard work by the research team, most archaeologists had still never heard of carbon-14. In 1949, Bill Libby decided to announce his discovery to the world. He chose a scientific meeting in New York. He was ready, he said, to test samples of unknown age and give them a close-to-accurate date.

Even before the news could get into scientific journals, scientists from the meeting began spreading it everywhere. Samples of bison bone, charcoal, seeds, sandals, and even coffins deluged the laboratory. They couldn't begin to test it all!

Headlines in newspapers all over the world screamed the news of the discovery. One reporter wrote that Dr. Libby "stumbled across" the discovery while working on something else. There was some truth to the comment, but according to *Time* magazine, the crew of students, who had been working for three years perfecting the idea, took offense. So, as a joke, they put up a sign in the lab reading: "On this spot W. F. Libby, 40, stumbled (for three years) on the carbon-14 dating method."

Naturally, some archaeologists were skeptical. They didn't know very much about chemistry, and they trusted it even less. The longer Libby's list of dated items grew, the more solidly they ignored it.

Finally, one spectacular result convinced most of the critics. Geologists and archaeologists had argued and agonized for many years over the time of the fourth Ice Age, which froze vast areas of North America and Northern Europe. Did it happen at the same time on both sides of the ocean? How long did it last? And, of course, how long ago did the great freeze happen?

There was no easy answer. Some geologists calculated the last huge glacier as forming 25,000 years ago. They based their guess on how long it took Niagara Falls to eat its way through miles of rock. Most archaeologists disagreed.

In 1950, researchers dug some ancient spruce logs out of the glacier's debris at Two Creeks, Wisconsin. Splinters of wood and peat moss from the prehistoric forest arrived at Bill Libby's lab to be analyzed.

Out came the special tweezers. The team removed all the specks of modern tree roots and mold. They cleaned and burned the spruce, to get at the ancient carbon.

Testing showed a surprise. The tree was only about 11,000 years old. The peat moss gave the same answer. And when other laboratories checked the results, their findings agreed.

Soon, bits of wood and other vegetation buried by the Ice Age across the Atlantic began to arrive from Scandinavia, England, Ireland, and Germany. They all gave the same 11,000-year-old date. Thanks to carbon-14 testing, geology had to change its whole outlook.

Once they knew what to look for, geologists and archaeologists could confirm the surprising results. Carbon-14 dating had solved a major mystery and earned a permanent place in the set of tools used to investigate the past.

But the story wasn't quite over. Some carbon-14 dates had always looked a bit suspicious to archaeologists, and others were definitely open to question. By 1961, it began to be obvious that Dr. Libby had made one serious error.

Bill Libby's early experiments had proved the carbon-14 level was the same all over the world. But had it *always* been exactly the same, going back thousands of years? There was no way to be certain.

Then, in 1967, another American scientist thought of a way. Dr. Hans E. Seuss (not the writer) combined carbon-14 dating with his own specialty of dendrochronology, the science of tree-ring counting.

Some trees live to be more than 4,000 years old. By relating the overlap of their rings to the ring patterns of ancient wood samples, dendrochronologists have pieced together a chronological line going back many thousands of years.

Dr. Seuss thought of measuring the carbon-14 levels in separate tree rings. He suspected they might not all be the same. And sure enough, they weren't. The carbon-14 levels were different for different years in the past. Sometimes they were different enough to throw radiocarbon dates off by hundreds of years!

To solve the problem, Seuss put together a chart showing the years when there was more or less carbon-14 in the air. Radiochemists began using it to correct their results.

New measuring techniques have improved radiocarbon dating even more. Instead of a few grams of ancient tree bark, for example, radiochemists now need only a few milligrams. That is a thousand times less. Instead of counting clicks or flashes of radiation, they now count radioactive atoms directly. The accuracy is so good that the date may be within ten years or so of perfect. And the new technique allows scientists to date objects much older than Libby's first method. Soon they may reach 70,000 years.

In 1960, Willard F. Libby received the Nobel Prize in Chemistry for his discovery of carbon-14 dating. His find opened the door to other kinds of "atomic clocks" that can be used to date materials hundreds of thousands of years old. It also brought together two widely separated fields of science. When a dust-covered archaeologist in jeans seals a fragment of ancient charcoal in a screw-top jar and mails it to a white-coated chemist in a laboratory full of elaborate instruments, the result combines the best of the old and the new.

10 The Clue in the Computer

When Dorothy Crowfoot Hodgkin slid a tiny, wine-colored crystal under her X-ray camera, the photographic plate came out with a beautiful design. The intricate pattern of lights and shadows looked like a designer's doily, but it didn't tell much about the crystal. Hodgkin felt a surge of disappointment. She had hoped it would be the key to solving a mystery.

For twenty years, since George Minot announced his liver cure for pernicious anemia, researchers had struggled to uncover the hidden substance that saved lives. In 1948 they found it, in some red, needlelike crystals of vitamin B_{12}. Vitamin B_{12} controlled pernicious anemia so well that one injection every few weeks could take the place of eating pounds and pounds of raw liver.

But the molecules inside those tiny crystals turned out to be a new mystery. They were so complex no chemist could understand them. In fact, no one really knew what the new vitamin was.

The fuzzy X-ray pictures, at first, gave Hodgkin only one clue.

Vitamin B_{12} molecules are huge. Chemists knew that already. But the British chemist-crystallographer had hoped to decipher the structure of the unusual molecule, using a method called X-ray crystallography. Looking at the first picture gave her a sinking feeling that the whole scheme was impossible.

Dorothy Crowfoot had been fascinated by crystals since 1920, when she learned to grow them in a summer science class. The ten-year-old girl was so interested she asked her teachers to let her study chemistry in school. Normally, only boys did.

Dorothy had been born in Egypt, and her archaeologist-father still lived there. On a visit from England, Dorothy learned to pan for gold. Instead of gold, she found a handful of shiny black crystals in the creek behind her Egyptian home. By the time thirteen-year-old Dorothy had identified the fascinating crystals, in the laboratory back at school, she was "hooked" on crystals for life.

But after graduation from Oxford University, in England, she ran into a problem. Women scientists were rare, and there seemed to be no openings for her in any kind of graduate program or job. The discouraged young chemist wasn't sure what to do next.

Then, riding a train across the English countryside, an old friend and professor of Dorothy's accidentally met another professor. They discussed her problem, and through them, she landed a place in the new X-ray crystallography laboratory at Cambridge.

There, Crowfoot learned to take pictures of crystals by passing X-ray beams through them onto a photographic plate. Electrons inside a crystal scatter, or diffract, the beams into beautiful patterns, and the angles of scattering can give clues about the

Dorothy Hodgkin

way atoms in the crystal are arranged. But making sense of the clues takes some complicated mathematics.

It was perfect work for Dorothy Crowfoot. She was a careful worker and good at math. Her vivid imagination let her see more in the diffraction pictures of crystals than others did.

The young crystallographer returned to Oxford and set up her own lab, in the dingy basement of a museum. She earned her doctorate and married a historian, Thomas Hodgkin. She soon gained a worldwide reputation for taking the clearest, most useful X-ray pictures possible and for knowing how to make those pictures show the structure of molecules.

So it was natural that the chemists who produced the first crystals of vitamin B_{12} would send a sample to Dr. Dorothy Hodgkin. But no one really thought she would be able to solve the whole mystery, just from the X-rays. No crystallographer had ever worked out the structure of a molecule half so complicated as vitamin B_{12} by crystallographic methods alone.

Meanwhile, "wet" chemists in several labs across England and the United States were trying to solve the mystery their own way, using test tubes and beakers. Mostly, they worked from the outside in, chipping off sections of the huge molecule, chemically, to see what they might be. And they ran tests on the whole molecule, to discover what kinds of atoms were inside.

Right away, the chemists got a surprise. Most large, organic molecules are made mainly of carbon, hydrogen, and oxygen, arranged in different ways. Most of vitamin B_{12}'s more than a hundred atoms were those same three light elements, as expected. But somewhere in the heart of the giant molecule, they found one atom of cobalt.

Cobalt is a heavy, bluish-white metal. What was it doing inside a vitamin? No one knew.

Dorothy Hodgkin didn't know why it was there, either, but it was a lucky find for her. She had already learned that one heavy atom, anywhere in a molecule, could be located on X-rays. Now her team had a starting point.

When they looked at the diffraction patterns of B_{12} again, Hodgkin and her assistants could make some order out of the hazy chaos. Because there, near the center, was the scatter pattern of a large, heavy atom. It had to be the cobalt. She and her team got to work.

The job was now possible, in theory. All they had to do was work from the center out, identifying the atoms next to cobalt and then the ones next to them, and so on. But in reality, the task looked overwhelming. Every calculation done pointed to dozens—even thousands—that needed to be done. Not many of Hodgkin's students felt enthusiastic about starting so much hard work.

Blackboards and pen-and-ink calculations bogged down right away. But Hodgkin already knew a better way. She had been doing some work with an old punch card mechanical calculator in the basement of a nearby building. The team began using it to sort their way through the mathematical mazes.

The trouble was, each calculation opened the way for so many others that the team was soon farther behind than when it started. There was no end in sight. It looked as if it might take hundreds of years to solve all the problems. Hodgkin's students had already spent several years and gotten almost no place.

At the same time, chemists studying B_{12} the ordinary way were also getting no place. They dissolved the molecule in acids and in bases and in alcohols. They filtered it and dried it and re-crystallized it thousands of times, learning a few details about the outermost atoms.

They even picked a chemical name for it, cyanocobalamin. But they were no closer to unlocking the whole structure. It was just too complicated!

As the "wet" chemists worked, they sometimes created new crystals that were slightly different from the mysterious B_{12}. These were something of a nuisance. So whenever that happened, the chemists packed up the crystals and shipped them to Dorothy Hodgkin. They were no use to the "wet" chemists, but they might be of interest to her.

Hodgkin X-rayed each sample and measured how it matched or was different from the original red crystals. They all produced hazy, mysterious patterns very much like vitamin B_{12}.

But they were not exactly like B_{12}. Every new crystal was unique in some way. And gradually, staring at the pictures hour after hour, Hodgkin began to see a clue to the mystery.

Deep inside, these new molecules were exactly like vitamin B_{12}. Each had a cobalt atom at the heart, surrounded by rings of other atoms. But some of the other atoms were different.

Comparing the shadowy patterns of one X-ray against another and another, Hodgkin began to pick out the different groups of atoms. Here was the cobalt, the same on every X-ray. And here were the rings of atoms surrounding it, sometimes the same and sometimes slightly different. She could see the characteristic patterns of nitrogen atoms, forming "bridges" from the cobalt to rings of carbon. And here was a carbon-nitrogen pair, sticking off by itself.

Other crystallographers have said Dorothy Hodgkin could

"see in stereo." Her mind began building a three-dimensional model of the complex molecule. It was "roughly spherical," or round in shape, she said, and it contained rings of atoms bridged together in four places. The ring of atoms around the cobalt lay in one plane, and another ring of atoms seemed to lie almost at right angles to it.

No wonder it has been so hard to figure out, she thought. It is not put together like any other molecule known. There is nothing else quite like it.

In Hodgkin's mind, the picture was almost clear. But proving it would not be easy. No one had ever used crystallography to solve such a difficult 3-D puzzle. And the stacks of calculations to be done just kept piling up—more work than the whole team could do in a lifetime.

The old punch card machine was not fast enough. Hodgkin needed something better. Then she thought of the new giant computers everyone was talking about.

It was now about 1953. Hodgkin and different groups of students had been working on the problem for five years. They needed help! The crystallographer began contacting computer scientists, to see if they could provide the kind of assistance she needed.

DEUCE and MARK I, the first computers she tried, were giant, room-sized pieces of equipment. They sounded "like a room full of ladies, knitting," as thousands of electrical relay "doors" clicked open and shut. The two solved problems ten times faster than the basement machine at Oxford, but that wasn't nearly fast enough. Hodgkin and her team fell farther behind.

Dorothy Hodgkin felt frustrated. The answer to the mystery

was clearly laid out in her head, but she began to think she would not live long enough to see all the necessary calculations done. Without those calculations as proof, the "stereo" picture in her head was just a fantasy.

Besides, what she could "see" was only the basic shape of the complicated molecule. Each specific atom's position on the structure was still lost in a haze of confusion. Unraveling every possibility was something like working a maze. They often spent weeks exploring "blind alleys," and every day made the situation look more hopeless.

Hodgkin didn't give up. Better and better computers were being built all the time. She kept looking for the perfect one. In 1954, Dorothy Hodgkin and her group teamed up with the best computer experts they could find—Dr. Kenneth Trueblood and students, using a computer named SWAC.

SWAC, in Los Angeles, California, did not have any clicking relays. It was too fast for that. Only a ripple of electricity had to move as information sped through its electronic "brain." There was no faster computer anywhere in the world.

Top computer speed was just what Hodgkin had been needing. Now her group could explore all the blind alleys they wanted. Now they could try out every possibility. The team got busy, putting all their data into shape.

It took more than a year, just to translate all that data into computer language. The whole process needed more than ten million separate calculations. But SWAC soon began pouring out answers as fast as the team could absorb them. By the end of the massive outpouring of information, they had pinpointed each atom of the vitamin B_{12} molecule precisely in space.

The final structure looked beautiful to Dorothy. It was almost exactly like the one she had seen in her head, years before.

Only a few outer atoms could not be positioned from the X-rays, and they had already been located by ordinary chemical methods. The final formula turned out to be $C_{63}H_{88}CoN_{14}O_{14}P$. (The letters stand for carbon, hydrogen, cobalt, nitrogen, oxygen, and phosphorus.)

By 1956, eight years after she had first examined the tiny red crystals, and thirty years after George Minot discovered the liver diet for pernicious anemia, Dorothy Hodgkin had solved the final part of the mystery. She called her victory, using crystallography, a "dreamlike situation."

Modern chemical mysteries are almost never solved by one person alone. Many people, too many to name, helped solve this one. But the most vital work was done in Dorothy Hodgkin's mind, and she received the 1964 Nobel Prize in Chemistry to honor her discovery.

More important than the chemical structure of one molecule, Hodgkin showed how X-ray crystallography, with the help of computers, can be used to unlock the structures of countless molecules that once seemed beyond anyone's power to understand. Solving the mystery of the complicated crystals brought chemistry into the computer age.

11 The Riddle

in Red

The best astronomers in the world admitted they were confused. The year was 1962, and strong radio signals seemed to be pouring out of certain spots in the sky. Yet when researchers trained their biggest telescopes on those spots, all they found were dim, ordinary-looking stars.

The longer astronomers studied those faint dots of light, the less ordinary they looked. In some ways, they didn't resemble stars at all. Since the whole field of astronomy was already in the midst of a confusing controversy, these puzzling "quasi-stellar sources" became a mystery within a mystery.

It all started with Albert Einstein's Theory of Relativity. The theory said the universe had to be expanding or contracting. In 1916, that sounded unbelievable, even to Einstein. "Everyone knew" that the universe never changed. Planets and comets might move around, but the stars stayed in their places.

Einstein tried juggling figures around, to "fix" his famous theory, so that the universe looked as stable on paper as it looked in the sky. Nothing worked. If the theory was right (and it seemed to be, in every other way), then everyone's idea about the universe had to be wrong. It was a mystery.

Clues were already coming in. In 1912, an American astronomer named Vesto Melvin Slipher took a spectrograph of a fuzzy, starlike object in the sky called the Andromeda nebula. It was called a nebula because scientists of the day didn't quite know what it was. Slipher saw the lines of familiar elements in its spectrum, but they were not in their proper places. The lines were shifted slightly to the blue-violet end of the rainbow spectrum, as if the length of their light waves had been shortened.

Motion can change the wavelength of light waves, Slipher knew, just as the motion of a train changes the sound of its whistle. The nebula must be moving. Slipher did some careful calculating and came up with the astonishing conclusion that Andromeda was rushing toward the earth at a speed of 700,000 miles per hour.

Some people who heard the news panicked. They thought the earth was in danger of a huge collision. They had no way of knowing that Andromeda is twelve trillion miles away. Other people simply thought Slipher was crazy.

Slipher took spectrographs of other objects in the sky. Their spectra were shifted, too, but in the other direction, toward the red end of the rainbow. They seemed to be moving away from earth at a fantastic rate. Slipher didn't know what to make of his strange findings.

It wasn't long before another American astronomer put two and two together. Edwin Powell Hubble did some measuring of his own, using the new 100-inch Hale telescope on Mount Wilson. It was up an eight-mile mule track out of Pasadena,

California, but Hubble used a motorcycle whenever he could. He rechecked all of Slipher's work and found only one mistake— Andromeda. Using some new information Slipher didn't have, Hubble recalculated and discovered that Andromeda is not careening toward earth, it is rushing away. In fact, *every object in the sky* outside of our own local galaxy is speeding away from earth. And the farther away they already are, the faster they are moving.

To Hubble, his findings neatly proved Einstein's theory. The red shift of all the stars in the universe means that the universe is expanding rapidly in all directions.

Hubble was a Rhodes scholar, a three-letter college athlete, and a graduate lawyer all before he decided to study astronomy. "It was astronomy that mattered," he said later.

Hubble quickly became a highly respected astronomer. He identified many of the starlike objects in the sky, such as Andromeda, as galaxies, or groups of stars like our own Milky Way. He put his findings about the red shift in the form of a natural law, which other astronomers could use to calculate speed and distance of faraway stars and galaxies. When he explained his theory, in a 1929 paper to the National Academy of Sciences, people listened.

But not everyone wanted to believe in an expanding universe. So the big controversy grew. Astronomers, physicists, other scientists, and people in general split into two factions over the mystery of the universe. How did it begin? What is it like? Where is it going?

Russian-American physicist and astronomer George Gamow headed one camp. He and his followers believed the universe began with a "Big Bang," some twelve billion years ago. All the matter and energy of the universe, collected into one huge "cosmic egg," exploded and set everything into motion. The universe is still expanding from the force of that explosion. Everything is moving away from everything else like dots on an expanding balloon or raisins in a rising loaf of bread.

But other scientists, headed by British mathematician Fred Hoyle, believed the universe has no beginning and no end. They called their theory "the Steady State," assuming the universe was, is now, and always will be the same in all directions. If the universe seems to be expanding, they said, it is only because new matter is constantly being created. Hoyle compared it to an overflowing bathtub with the faucet running. As galaxies move away from earth, new ones develop to fill the gaps. The rate of growth is, unfortunately, too slow and too small to measure.

No one knew how to resolve the controversy. A scientist traveling in a time machine could find the answer easily. If the universe looks the same in the past, present, and future, then the Steady State must be true. But if galaxies are closer together or farther apart or look or act differently in the past or future, then the Big Bang wins out.

Without a time machine, however, there seemed to be no way to solve the mystery of the universe. And since there was no proof either way, both sides enjoyed the argument. Then, in 1963, a special kind of "time machine" was discovered.

Clue #1—In 1931, Karl Jansky, at the Bell Telephone Laboratories, noticed radio waves coming from the sky. No other scientists seemed interested at the time.

Clue #2—During World War II, radarmen scanning the

sky for enemy planes kept finding background static they couldn't identify.

Clue #3—After the war, scientists began using military technology to study the sky. They found radio sources in every direction, but it was hard to pin them down to a precise location.

Clue #4—Radio astronomers pinpointed the first nine radio sources from the sky. But optical astronomers were disappointed. Their telescopes found small, faint, bluish stars in all nine locations. These nine stars had been on charts for years, but they looked too dim and unimportant to bother about.

Meanwhile, a young Dutch astronomer, born the same year Hubble explained the red shift, was studying the sky. Maartin Schmidt was in love with astronomy. When he was twelve, an uncle helped him build a telescope that reflected stars onto his bedroom mirror. By the time Maartin was in high school, he knew so much astronomy the teacher asked him to take over that part of the science class.

When Maartin finished college, the Carnegie Institution offered him a fellowship to spend a year working with astronomers in the United States. And by the time he had finished his training, the California Institute of Technology invited him back to stay. Maartin packed up his wife and family and moved from Holland to the United States.

Dr. Maartin Schmidt's specialty was looking through telescopes. His sharp, dark eyes could spot interesting things other people missed. But Cal Tech assigned him to take over for a retiring professor who was studying radio waves. The professor had been cataloging the mysterious "quasi-steller sources" of radio static, trying to match them up with points of light from

Courtesy of the California Institute of Technology

Maartin Schmidt

his telescope. He had about a hundred matches lined up. But the evidence was vague and confusing.

The points of light were confusing, too. For years, astronomers had thought they were small, dim stars. But why were they shooting off noisy radio waves? Nearby stars don't give off radio waves, and these stars were too small and dim to be faraway galaxies. The whole thing didn't make sense.

It didn't make sense to Schmidt, either, as he took over the research. And other astronomers on the project were far ahead of the Dutch newcomer.

There was Alan Sandage, for instance, who had discovered the first "quasi-stellar source." He and Jesse Greenstein, head of the astronomy department, had put in hours of work passing "quasi-starlight" through their spectroscopes, with no results. Then Greenstein had an idea. Maybe the light was just too dim to register. He set up a seven-hour exposure of one pinpoint of light named 3C-48, from its listing in the third Cambridge catalog of radio sources.

This time, he got something. But it was disappointing. On the tiny filmstrip, less than an inch long, no rainbow colors showed at all. The photograph had picked up just a few tiny black and white lines.

When Greenstein studied the unimposing photographs carefully under a microscope, they turned out to be more interesting than they first looked. The lines he had photographed didn't match anything he had ever seen before.

He compared them to spectrographs of all the known elements, especially the ones commonly found in stars, such as hydrogen, helium, magnesium, and so on. No matches. What could it mean?

Were the lines spectra of new elements not found on earth? The astronomer didn't think so. He knew chemists are sure they recognize all the possible elements now, except for some very large, unstable atoms. Those would not be likely to be the main components of a star. So, what else could the lines mean?

Greenstein had an idea. Sometimes very hot, "excited" atoms throw off unusual spectral lines. In fact, this spectrum looked a little like the spectra of fireballs from hydrogen bombs. They might be the dense, nearby remains of exploding stars. He wrote his ideas into a carefully worded paper to send to a scientific magazine.

Meanwhile, in Australia, astronomer Cyril Hazard thought of a new way to pinpoint the exact location of one "quasi-stellar source." His team picked one called 3C-273, which was directly in the path of the moon.

As the moon passed in front of 3C-273 one night in late 1962, the Australians measured the exact moment the radio crackle stopped. When the moon moved away, they noted the exact time the radio noise began again. Since astronomers know precisely where the moon is at all times, Hazard could calculate exactly what spot in the sky the moon covered and uncovered at those times. He published its location in a scientific journal.

When Schmidt read about it, he felt excited. This was just what he had been waiting for: a newly discovered "quasi-stellar source" of his own. He got out old charts and maps of that part of the sky and began to search them thoroughly.

Schmidt's eyes, used to years of peering through telescopes, spotted something right away. There was a dim, bluish star in the exact place the Australians had said something would be. It had been like an ordinary dot of light.

The star was not new. It had been listed in catalogs for almost a hundred years. But no one had ever bothered to study it in detail.

Schmidt needed better pictures. He put on a heavy, heated fllght suit, like the kind astronauts wear, and rode the elevator to the top of the huge Hale 200-inch telescope, on Mount Palomar. He loaded the cameras and sat down to wait until dawn, playing classical music on the radio. Schmidt liked to stay in touch with his equipment, and he could scan the freezing sky for clouds that might spoil his pictures.

In the best photographs the big telescope could take, 3C-273 looked like a fuzzy lollipop on a stick. It was a two-part source. The round area was brightest, but most of the radio signal came from the second section, a hazy, protruding jet. It didn't look much like a star, but it was too compact to be a galaxy. Schmidt didn't know what it was.

Now, he needed a spectrograph. He knew how hard his colleagues had been working to record the spectra of these strange "quasi-stellar" objects, so he took special care. Using Greenstein's technique, Schmidt took a long exposure of 3C-273.

On a tiny piece of film, Schmidt got a strange pattern of five black and white lines. Like Greenstein's spectrum, it didn't seem to match anything. Maartin stared at the lines under his microscope. He had no idea what they meant.

For six weeks, he mulled the problem over in his mind. Even when he was watching television or playing the violin, the problem haunted him. What could the strange lines be?

In February, 1963, Maartin Schmidt decided to write a paper describing his find, but offering no explanation. And as he wrote, an idea popped into his mind. Three of the lines were spaced just like hydrogen's familiar spectral "fingerprint."

But hydrogen couldn't be right. The hydrogen lines on a dim star ought to be in the blue region of the spectrum, and these were way over in the red.

Just to make sure, he matched his lines against a normal hydrogen spectrum. The lines fitted perfectly, and the other two lines matched bands of color for oxygen and magnesium. But they showed a red shift of 16 percent!

Schmidt did some fast calculations. A red shift that great indicated a star 1,500,000,000 light-years away. (Astronomers sometimes measure distance by how far light can travel in a year; 1.5 billion light-years is about 90 trillion miles.) If that were true, 3C-273 was farther from earth than almost any other object in the sky!

"That night," Schmidt told *National Geographic*, later, "I went home in a state of disbelief. I said to my wife, 'Something really incredible happened to me today.' "

It still didn't make sense. A star that far away would be too small to see, even with the 200-inch telescope Schmidt was using. Something had to be wrong.

The confused astronomer thought of another proof. One of the familiar lines of hydrogen was missing from his film. The red shift was so great that the line called H-alpha could have been shifted clear off the rainbow into the region beyond visible light. But if the spectrum were really hydrogen, that line had to exist. It ought to be just off the chart, in the region scientists call infrared. A special camera could record it.

Maartin Schmidt did not have an infrared camera set up, but he knew of another astronomer who had already taken the kind of pictures he needed. He called Dr. Beverly Oke. Oke checked his own collection of photographs. Sure enough, on every shot, just at the place Schmidt had said it ought to be, was a dark H-alpha band.

There was no longer any doubt. Schmidt had identified the mysterious spectral lines as ordinary hydrogen. They came from a "quasi-stellar" object, however, that was anything but ordinary. It had to be an unbelievable distance away. And if it were really shining from that far away, then the "faint little star" had to be one of the brightest objects in the universe! The discovery left him, as he told *Time* reporters, "in a complete state of shock."

When Jesse Greenstein heard the news, he rushed to his own microscope. The tiny black and white spectrum of 3C-48 began to look like hydrogen, too. But his red-shifted 36 percent, more than twice as far as Schmidt's. His "quasi-star" seemed to be 3.6 billion light-years away.

On Greenstein's desk was the paper he had planned to publish. Quickly, he put it away. "If it weren't for Maartin," he said in *Time* magazine, "I could have been caught with my scientific trousers down."

When Schmidt's paper was published, the race began among astronomers to find out as much as possible, as quickly as possible, about the strange "quasi-stellar sources." If the enormous red shifts were really true, then "quasi-stars" might be the "time machine" to the past that astronomers had been seeking.

Hong-Yee Chiu, an American physicist, coined a catchier name for the mysterious objects. He called them "quasars." Most astronomers hated the name, but the press loved it. Soon quasars were making headlines across the world.

The new facts coming in were as astonishing as the first. Some quasars were eight to ten billion light-years away. They were smaller in size than a galaxy, but brighter than a hundred galaxies. Each gave off radio signals ten million times stronger than the whole Milky Way. And the farther astronomers looked, the more of them there seemed to be. It looked as if, ten billion years ago, quasars must have filled the universe!

Big Bang proponents were elated. The "time machine" seemed to be proving their theory.

Steady State believers felt discouraged. Their only hope was to prove Maartin Schmidt wrong. The red shift was real, they admitted, but what if it weren't caused by motion? What if something else made the tiny lines shift across the spectrum? What if quasars were really small, nearby stars, after all?

Hoyle and the others tried several theories. Perhaps quasars were the remains of giant explosions. Perhaps quasars were objects "thrown out" of nearby galaxies at high speed.

One by one, astronomers studied the theories and disproved them. Maartin Schmidt worked hardest on the last one. If quasars were being ejected from nearby galaxies, surely some of them would be flying toward earth, instead of away. Those ought to have a high blue shift. Schmidt searched spectrum after spectrum. No blue shift. And some ought to be shooting off sideways. They would change position. He searched old and new charts. No quasar moved sideways.

In several places, astronomers could see quasars through the haze of closer galaxies. That was proof enough for most scientists that quasars are really as far away as their red shift indicates.

Finally, in 1965, the Steady State faction gave up. It was, according to *Newsweek* magazine, as if then President Lyndon Johnson had announced his resignation from the Democratic

Party. "It seems likely," wrote Hoyle, in *Nature* magazine, "that the [Steady State] idea will have to be discarded."

There was other evidence Hoyle cited, but quasars were the main unsolvable problem. They are "relics," he said, of a time when the universe was different. Because of the "time machine" Maartin Schmidt discovered, every theory of the origin of the universe now includes a Big Bang.

Quasars, themselves, are still a mystery. Astronomers and physicists still hope to discover what gives them the fantastic energy to shine as brightly as they do. Learning more about quasars may help solve other ancient mysteries of the universe.

12 The Case of the
Little Green Men

In a Nancy Drew mystery book, the young detective usually grapples with two separate puzzles which turn out to help solve each other. In 1967, a young researcher named Jocelyn Bell uncovered a real-life mystery that puzzled astronomers all over the world—until they added another unsolved mystery more than nine hundred years old.

Jocelyn Bell had always wanted to be an astronomer. As a little girl, she sometimes talked with scientists at the planetarium near her home in Northern Ireland. But one thing bothered her. She could never manage to keep awake until very late, and all her friends at the observatory had told her that staying up all night was an important part of an astronomer's job.

Then Jocelyn learned about a new kind of astronomy. It searched, not for light from distant stars and galaxies, but for another kind of radiation from outer space called microwaves. Microwaves are waves of energy a million times longer than light waves. In fact, they are very much like short radio waves, and the scientists who study them are called radio astronomers.

130

About the time Bell was graduated from college, a new project in radio astronomy was getting under way at the Mullard Radio Astronomy Observatory outside Cambridge University in England. The study seemed especially designed for her: almost all the work was done in the daytime. Bell joined the crew as a graduate student researcher.

The huge radio telescope took two years to build. It consisted of 2,048 radio receivers, spaced out over an area larger than four football fields. With it, there was no need to peer through a lens at the sky, because the waves the telescope picked up could not be seen. Instead, automatic instruments connected to the receivers translated data into three wavy lines traced onto graph paper.

Jocelyn Bell's job was to analyze those tracings. The huge radio telescope put out almost a hundred feet of data every day, and she studied it all carefully, picking out sources of microwaves from different parts of the sky and charting their locations.

This project was to be Jocelyn Bell's thesis, the research paper graduate students must write to earn an advanced degree. But she had other work to do, and the charts took too much time. She kept getting behind, sometimes weeks behind.

Local static from car ignitions, thermostats, refrigerators, and sometimes even police cars made her job more difficult. Radio waves from outer space are so weak that a radio telescope must be extra-sensitive. That sensitivity causes it to record all kinds of man-made interference. But Bell soon learned to tell which squiggles on the blue-lined paper were really from space and which came from the surrounding countryside.

Then one day in October, she found something unusual, as she was catching up on some old charts. A funny blip appeared on an August chart that didn't look like anything she had seen before. It certainly wasn't the kind of signal she was supposed to be studying, but it didn't quite look like local interference, either. Jocelyn couldn't figure out what it might be.

Six more times on the charts from August to the end of September, Bell found this same mysterious "blip," which she called a "bit of scruff." It always appeared in a constellation called Vulpecula, the "little fox."

Bell showed the strange tracings to Anthony Hewish, the director of her project. He was puzzled, too. They decided to give the blip a closer look.

The simplest way to examine a particular section of graph made by a tracing pen is to run the instrument faster. That spreads out the lines and makes them easier to study. But the speed-up adjustment had to be done by hand, at just the right moment.

Jocelyn went out to the observatory right before Vulpecula was due to appear and switched the recorder onto high speed. But nothing happened. The pen traced a normal pattern for that part of the sky.

Day after day, Jocelyn watched the high-speed tracings move in a steady pattern. No blips, no confusion, no mystery.

Finally, Bell skipped a day to hear a special lecture. When she went out to pick up the graphs for that day, there was the mysterious blip. "It's back," she told Hewish on the phone.

The next day, Jocelyn made sure she was at the telescope in time to speed up the recorder, and this time she caught the elusive blip. In fact, it turned out to be a series of blips, evenly spaced about one and one-third seconds apart.

At first, she was disappointed and suspicious. Magnified by

Jocelyn Bell and Dr. Anthony Hewish

the high speed, the tracings began to look just like the kind made by a man-made signal generator. Jocelyn wondered if some of the men at the lab were playing a trick on her.

Bell explained her suspicions to Dr. Hewish. "Oh, well, that settles it," he said. "It must be man-made."

But scientists are always curious. Neither the young student nor the experienced astronomer could give up until they had solved the mystery, even if it only meant finding out who was playing the joke.

The next day, Dr. Hewish came out to the observatory to see the puzzling blip. Jocelyn was worried. There had been so many days when it did not appear.

But there it was, right on schedule, spaced out by the high-speed tracing: a series of mysterious marks on the graph, 1.33730113 seconds apart, from a spot in the sky where no microwaves ought to be.

There the real mystery began. Someone might have tried to play a joke on a pig-tailed female graduate student, but no one would try that kind of trick on Dr. Hewish. So the puzzling blips had to be real. But what were they?

The blips were pulsing much too frequently to be from a star. Stars are huge. They might produce bursts of microwaves every few hours as they spin their massive bulk, but not every second.

Whatever was causing the blips had to be something small— much, much smaller than a star. In fact, it seemed obvious that the blips had to be coming from somewhere on earth, except for one more confusing detail Bell had noticed. The blips were operating on star time, not earth time.

To astronomers, the "day" is not quite the twenty-four hours most people know. It is only twenty-three hours and fifty-six minutes. So things that happen on star time happen four minutes earlier each earth day. And that is exactly how the blip was behaving. Every day it pulsed four minutes sooner than it had the day before. "So," as Jocelyn Bell said later, "if it was Joe Bloggs going home from work in a badly suppressed car, he was getting home about four minutes earlier each night."

But if it wasn't a car and wasn't local interference, what could it be? Was it the equipment? They checked everything. Finally they used another telescope to scan the same spot in the sky. It recorded the same mysterious blip. That ruled out a mistake.

About that time, someone suggested that the signal might be coming from another civilization trying to contact earth. Partly joking and partly serious, the scientists in Hewish's group named the blip LGM-1, for "little green men."

Astronomers are always skeptical of flying saucer stories, but this time they were not so sure. If there really were "little green men" somewhere in outer space, they would live on a planet. Planets are small, and they move with the stars, but they don't give off microwaves all by themselves. Maybe, just possibly, the mysterious signal from space *was* a message from living creatures on another planet. "Those weeks in December, 1967," Dr. Hewish said later, "were the most exciting in my life."

They were not quite so exciting for Jocelyn Bell. In fact, they were downright annoying. She was trying to earn her Ph.D. by charting and identifying microwaves from outer space, and these strange, unexplainable "bits of scruff" were confusing all her data. To make matters even worse, she was way behind, again, in analyzing the charts. It was just before Christmas vacation, but everything seemed to be going wrong.

That same evening, Jocelyn went out to the lab to try and

catch up. Just before closing time, she was startled to find another blip on a chart from a different part of the sky.

Bell began thumbing back through hundreds of feet of blue-lined paper. Yes, the new blip had appeared several times before. And, strangely, it was almost time for the telescope to scan that exact part of the sky.

Bell badly wanted a high-speed tracing of the new blip. It was bitterly cold outside, and the radio telescope did not receive well on a cold night. At first, she could not get the receiver to work at all. She tried breathing hot air onto the apparatus. She even tried kicking it and swearing at it. Finally, the scope began to receive, for about five minutes.

But to Jocelyn Bell's relief, it worked for just the right five minutes. The graph paper showed a spaced-out tracing of the new blip. Bell had to stay awake most of the night, but this time she didn't feel like falling asleep. She had discovered another key to the puzzle. Jocelyn named the new blip, with pulses one and one-fourth seconds apart, LGM-2.

Soon after that, two more pulsing blips were discovered. They were named LGM-3 and 4, but by that time the group had almost given up on the idea that the signals were messages from little green men or people of any other shape or color. It didn't seem very likely that intelligent creatures in four different parts of the sky would be beaming the same kind of signal in earth's direction. And even though the signals were weak, they were using up an incredible amount of energy. No civilization would be likely to waste so much energy when they didn't even know whom they were contacting.

Finally, if the signals were coming from a planet, they should change slightly as the planet revolved around its own sun. They didn't. So, to get rid of the slightly embarrassing idea of "little green men," the scientists changed the name of the blips from LGMs to "pulsars." The name matched the mysterious "quasars," discovered just a few years before.

Now the mystery was back to the start: not from a star, not from earth, not from little green men on distant planets. Anthony Hewish began haunting the library, looking for an answer. And there, he found another mystery.

This mystery was first recorded in 1054, in China. A royal astronomer named Yang Wei-t'e observed a "guest star" that appeared where no star had been seen before. It was so bright it could be seen in the daytime, but in just over a year, it disappeared completely.

Modern astronomers identified the "guest star" as a supernova, which is a huge star that blows up suddenly, spewing radiation as bright as a million suns.

Fred Zwicky, an astronomer at the California Institute of Technology in the 1930s, was interested in supernovas. He wanted to see one, but supernovas are rare. A supernova as clear and close as the one in 1054 may only happen once or twice in a thousand years. So Zwicky began looking in galaxies far distant from earth. He couldn't find a single star where any supernova had been thought to be. It seemed that once their spectacular brilliance dimmed, they were gone forever.

Zwicky and his colleague, Walter Baade, began to wonder why that should be. Certainly, most of the material in the star must have been turned into energy by the gigantic explosion. But what happened to the matter left over? It was a mystery.

Zwicky and Baade thought of a solution to their mystery. They reasoned that the force of the star's explosion would squeeze the inner core of the star. Gravity would squeeze it even tighter until the atoms inside began to collapse. Since atoms are mostly empty space, the collapsed atoms in a star millions of miles across could be compressed by gravity into a dense ball no more than twenty miles across.

Zwicky named these strange, collapsed stars he had imagined "neutron stars," because the compressed atoms would have turned into particles called neutrons. A neutron star would be much smaller than the moon, but its gravity would be so strong that a tablespoonful of material would weigh more than a hundred million tons.

But Zwicky could not prove that his solution to the mystery of supernovas was correct, because there was no way to look for neutron stars. A few astronomers tried; none had any success. Radio telescopes had not yet been invented.

Anthony Hewish read about neutron stars in the library at Cambridge. He had heard of them before, but now they sounded like just what he was looking for: something much smaller than an ordinary star, moving with the stars, that might be giving off energy in the form of microwaves. Hewish felt very sure he had solved both mysteries. Pulsars and neutron stars must be the same thing.

But being sure is not scientific proof. Hewish, Bell, and the rest of the staff announced the discovery of pulsars to the world in February, 1968, using neutron stars as a possible explanation.

Immediately, radio astronomers everywhere began to look for pulsars. By the end of 1968, more than twenty had been discovered, several of them where supernovas had been expected to be. One pulsar was in a part of the sky called the Crab Nebula—right where the famous "guest star" had been seen.

That was almost, but not quite, enough proof that pulsars are really neutron stars. Two more bits of evidence were needed.

Thomas Gold, an astronomer at Cornell University, provided one bit. He explained the flashes of radiation from a pulsar by suggesting that neutron stars spin faster and faster as they collapse, like a skater who folds her arms close to her body as she twirls. The spin wraps a magnetic blanket tightly around them, holding all the leftover energy inside.

But at the poles, or the North-South points of a neutron star, the magnetic blanket is not so tight. A thin beam of radiation is able to escape. And if that beam is pointed in the direction of earth, we get a flash each time the star spins around.

But, Gold added, as energy escapes, the pulsars should eventually begin to slow down. When astronomers checked very, very carefully, they found that Gold was correct. Pulsars are slowing down, about a billionth of a second a day.

"How fantastically stupid we really are," Gold said later, not to have thought of this kind of evidence sooner.

For the final proof, astronomers at an observatory in Arizona set up a carefully designed experiment to try and *see* a pulsar. They used a telescope that could "collect" light until it had enough to show very faint stars on a screen, and they aimed for the pulsar in the Crab Nebula.

On January 15, 1969, conditions were perfect. When all the apparatus was turned on, a line of green dots began to climb across the screen. Astronomers were actually seeing light from Yang Wei-t'e's "guest star" for the first time in 914 years.

In 1974, Anthony Hewish and Sir Martin Ryle, who had developed the radio antenna used in the discovery of pulsars, were awarded the Nobel Prize in Physics. (Many scientists feel that Jocelyn Bell should have received a share of the prize, too, even though she was Hewish's student.)

More than 300 pulsars are now known. The solution to "The Case of the Little Green Men" did not locate any life on other planets, but it produced a whole new field of research into the way stars decay.

13 The Mystery of the

Missing Uranium, Case 2

Uranium is one of the most valuable elements on earth. So when French nuclear engineers noticed samples of expensive ore that were missing part of their uranium, the scientists grew alarmed. Where had the lost atoms gone? Had a clever thief stolen them? Or was the measuring equipment failing? No one knew.

In nature, most uranium atoms are slightly radioactive and have 92 protons and 146 neutrons in their nucleus. Scientists call these atoms uranium-238 (92 + 146 = 238).

But the really valuable, highly radioactive atom of uranium is uranium-235, with three fewer neutrons. The atom that fissions best is ^{235}U. It is the isotope that fuels nuclear power plants. It makes up almost exactly 0.7202 percent of all uranium —less than 1 percent. And ^{235}U is the kind of uranium that was mysteriously missing from the French ore.

Isotopes are atoms of the same element, which have different numbers of neutrons, like almost-identical twins. They are always difficult to separate, because, chemically, they are just alike. But nuclear engineers have found ways to isolate the rare uranium-235 atoms from the more common uranium-238, by taking advantage of their slightly lighter weight.

In nuclear refinery plants all over the world, engineers enrich ordinary uranium, adding extra ^{235}U atoms to it, until they get a 3 percent ^{235}U level—the level needed in nuclear power plants. But in 1972, an engineer at the Pierrelatte refinery, in France, uncovered a mystery.

H. Bouzigues' job sounded simple. The French engineer was supposed to analyze samples of ^{235}U-enriched uranium hexa-fluoride gas to see exactly how much ^{235}U they contained. He used an instrument called a mass spectrometer, which electri-fies molecules of gas, speeds them up, and then measures how much their path is curved by a magnet. Lighter atoms of uranium-235 curve more than heavier uranium-238. The in-strument did most of the work, while Bouzigues wrote down the answers it gave.

But on June 7, something went wrong. Bouzigues prepared a new standard sample for the spectrometer to measure enriched samples against. He took fresh, unconcentrated uranium, straight from the refinery's supply, carefully measured an exact amount of it and checked it against the old uranium standard. The two did not match.

Bouzigues could not believe his eyes. Instead of the normal 0.7202 percent, the new standard read 0.7171 percent.

The difference was less than four parts in a thousand, but it stunned all the scientists in the lab. They knew natural uranium always has the same proportion of uranium-235 to uranium-238 within one part in a thousand, from Colorado to Czechoslovakia. Even uranium in the moon rocks brought back by American

astronauts measured the same. Most scientists think the pro-
portions were set when the earth was formed.

So why should this one sample be so mysteriously different?
Like any good scientist, the first thing Bouzigues did was start
over and recheck everything. But every time he repeated the
analysis, he got the same, strange answer.

Maybe, Bouzigues reasoned, there was something wrong with
the uranium he was using. If it had gotten mixed with the
"tailings" from the concentration process—the leftover ^{238}U—
then its concentration of ^{235}U would naturally be less. Maybe it
wasn't as pure as he had thought. But when he tried several
more samples, as pure as the plant could supply, they all
measured low.

As soon as he was sure there was no mistake on his part,
Bouzigues took his problem to his bosses, the officials of the
French Commissariat à l'Energie Atomique (CEA). Something
is wrong with this uranium, he reported. Somehow, part of the
^{235}U seems to have disappeared.

The CEA officials took Bouzigues' report very seriously. They
couldn't afford to let a rare and costly resource slip away without
a trace. The agency appointed a team of scientists to look into
the mystery.

In the past, scientific mysteries were usually solved by one
person, working alone. The modern way is a group of experts,
working separately on different parts of a puzzle. The CEA team
included minerologists, nuclear physicists, and isotopic chemists,
all following the unusual ore's trail.

Part of the team started by examining every drum of ore at the
processing plant, where the uranium oxide in the ore is turned
into gas. The samples they tested were *all* too low, even the ore

just unloaded off the ship from Africa. Could all of it be contaminated?

Impossible. Pierrelatte's plant was running smoothly. The
problem was in the ore itself, not in the plant. No one knew
why.

The uranium oxide brought into a refinery is called "yellow
cake." Researchers traced the particular shipment of powdery
yellow ore Bouzigues had sampled to a mill called Mounana, in
southwestern Gabon, Africa.

Meanwhile, other team members took a side trip to the
United States, carrying lead-shielded samples of the mysterious
uranium with them. At the National Bureau of Standards, in
Washington, D.C., scientists compared their low-reading samples
directly with the best U.S. uranium ore standards, using American laboratory equipment. The results did not match.

At least, now they could be sure the French equipment was
not failing. And there was nothing wrong with French methods
or French standard samples. But something unexplained was
very wrong with this particular uranium.

Next, the African team took over. Here, the mystery deep-
ened. Traveling over the mountains to the mill at Mounana,
they learned a new, horrifying fact: the ore they were tracing
was not the only ore low in precious ^{235}U.

The more completely they checked, the more alarmed they
became. Mounana mill had saved a small sample of every batch
of ore ever processed. And for *two years*, the scientists discovered, many of the ores had been running strangely low in
^{235}U. The team gave up the idea of a "clever thief." Not even
an organized gang could steal so much hard-to-separate material
from so much rock.

The Oklo uranium mine, site of the natural nuclear reactor

The mystery affected more than 700 tons of ore. As the scientists began calculating, they realized that the missing uranium
was a far greater problem than anyone had thought. It wasn't
just a curious shortage in Bouzigues' laboratory anymore; it
involved more than 200 kilograms (440 pounds) of the precious,
fissionable uranium—enough to power as many French homes
and factories as 500 million liters (140 million gallons) of oil.

While some team members were calculating losses, others
were carefully sifting the mill's records. Mounana served two
mines, but all the defective ore came from one place—a mine
called Oklo.

The next step was a visit to the mysterious mine. Oklo was
now a huge, open pit in the African rock and clay, at the site
of an ancient river delta. Hundreds of tons of ore had already
been dug out of the gaping hole and hauled away. In fact,
miners were busy loading and removing ore when the scientists
arrived. Learning anything valuable from the ugly pit seemed
hopeless.

Most of the site was gone, but a major clue remained. Before
digging began, mining engineers had surveyed a carefully
measured "checkerboard" pattern across the site and drilled
out core samples of rock from each point on the grid.

The cores were safely in storage. They could be tested. But
when the team looked for them, it turned out that they were
stored in France. So the mystery moved back across the ocean.

In France, technicians removed the stored, radioactive rock
and analyzed it. Most of the samples tested normal.

But two of the early samples showed the slight uranium-235
depletion the team was looking for. One sample, taken from
the richest vein, right where miners were now digging, measured

only 0.44 percent ^{235}U—just over half the normal amount.

The samples with the most total uranium always held the least uranium-235. Researchers had already discovered that strange fact in the mill samples. But now they could use the information to pinpoint the lowest actual spot.

Then they uncovered another surprise. A few core samples showed *too much* ^{235}U. The concentration had actually increased! It was as if the "thief" had been playing "Robin Hood," by taking from the richest ore and giving to the poor.

While some technicians were examining the uranium levels, others carried out different tests on the same rock cores. They were looking for clues, and they found them.

The samples that were lacking the most uranium made up for it with high concentrations of other elements—unusual elements that were barely found at all in the surrounding rock or in normal ore. The searchers found atoms of neodymium, samarium, europium, cerium, and other odd elements, and they appeared in unusual forms not often found anywhere in nature. But they looked and acted exactly as leftover products do inside a man-made nuclear reactor.

After three months, the team began comparing notes. A wild, unbelievable idea, that had been at the back of their minds all along, now began to look less ridiculous. In fact, it had become the likeliest answer. The French scientists had discovered a natural nuclear reactor. The missing uranium had been used as fuel for a "power plant" buried deep under the African earth.

As far as the team was concerned, the mystery was solved. In late 1972, they announced their discovery to the world.

A few American scientists were elated at the news. They had predicted years before that a natural reactor was possible.

Others were not so sure. Years of hard work and scientific skill had gone into developing nuclear reactors. How could something so complex happen spontaneously? And if it had, wouldn't it have left some outward sign, such as a blown-up mountain?

Still, facts were facts. "I haven't been able to think of any better explanation," said Nobel Prize-winning Dr. Glenn Seaborg. Other scientists thought it was just as logical to assume a spaceship set down at Oklo, took on fresh fuel, and dumped its nuclear wastes. They needed more proof.

The French determined to find it. They appointed Roger Naudet to head up Project Franceville, named for the town closest to the mine. His job: find the proof.

The French physicist laid his plans carefully. Naudet knew a great deal about nuclear reactors and what makes them work. But he knew that wouldn't be enough. He expanded the original team to include experts on everything from ancient geology to nuclear chemistry. Then, in March, 1973, he and part of the group flew to Gabon.

They landed at Libreville, on the African coast. A flight over the tropical rain forests took them to Franceville, and they drove out to the mine.

Work had stopped. The mining company agreed to give the scientists a chance to collect whatever facts they could, quickly, before heavy machinery hauled all the evidence away.

Clues were everywhere, to the trained eyes looking. The sandstone wall of the pit showed ripple marks, signs of ancient water flowing through clay. Bright yellow patches of unmined uranium stood out starkly against the light brown sandstone, showing the size and shape of the veins of ore. The color showed the presence of oxygen, since unoxidized uranium is usually black. The experts took note of all the clues they saw, and got to work on the ones that interested them most.

The reactor, itself, was the main thing. Naudet and his group located at least four reactor sites, two of them not yet mined. With the help of his experts, Naudet checked all four sites against the five major factors needed to build a nuclear reactor.

As related in Chapter 7 "The Mystery of the Missing Uranium, Case 1," Otto Hahn discovered that a uranium-235 atom can split when it is struck by a neutron. As it splits, it gives off two or three neutrons of its own.

It did not take scientists long, after Hahn's discovery, to speculate about what might happen if those newly released neutrons hit other uranium atoms. That could cause them to split, too, and then their neutrons could cause more to split, and so on. Uranium fissioning could cause a chain reaction that keeps itself going, with no more energy added.

The scientists were right. They did develop a chain reaction that led to the first atomic bomb and to all the peaceful uses of nuclear power that followed. Now, Naudet's scientists were trying to prove that nature had done the same thing, with no human help, some two billion years ago.

So Roger Naudet outlined the five steps and let his expert "detectives" fill in how nature might have accomplished them. To build a nuclear reactor, it takes:

1. Enough ^{235}U—Today, engineers have to concentrate the ^{235}U to get 3 percent. That is the most difficult part of their work. But uranium-235 has a half-life of seven hundred million years, and it has been disappearing since the world began. Two billion years ago, when the natural reactor was operating,

uranium had a much higher natural concentration of ^{235}U. In
fact, for years, physicists have joked that it would have been
easy for a prehistoric "physicist" to build a reactor. All he or
she would have had to do was get enough uranium together
and the reaction would start.

2. Enough uranium (both kinds)—Today, traces of uranium
are found in rocks everywhere, but concentrating it is difficult.
Two billion years ago conditions were different. Oxygen from
tiny plants was just finding its way into the air. That oxygen
may have turned black, prehistoric uranium into the yellow,
dissolving form. Ancient rivers carried it deep underground
where it changed back to the black form and stayed, building
up thick pockets of rich ore. Conditions around Oklo were just
right for that to happen.

3. Suitable shape—So that neutrons do not escape, modern
engineers design reactors with a uranium core at least half a
meter thick in all directions. Geologists found that nature had
"designed" the uranium veins at Oklo to be easily thick enough.
Some were three hundred times thicker than they needed to be.

4. No "poisons"—In modern reactors, the uranium is puri-
fied. All other elements that might soak up neutrons and
"poison" the chain reaction have been removed. At Oklo,
chemists found none of the most common "poisons." The reaction had an "all clear" from nature to begin.

5. Finally, a moderator—As Fermi and Hahn and Meitner
discovered, slow neutrons fission better than fast ones. Neutrons
fly out of splitting uranium too fast to split other atoms, but
physicists learned ways to slow them down. One good way is to
add water. At Oklo, nature chose the same method. Water
trickling through cracks in the rocks made a perfect moderator.

And the water method explained why the mountain never blew up. Whenever the reaction got too hot, the water boiled away and the chain closed down. As the water came back, it started again, over and over for millions of years.

Naudet's team spent several years collecting these and other clues. They even explained why some of the mysterious ore had extra uranium-235. The "Robin Hood" effect happened because ^{235}U can sometimes be a waste product of a fission chain. The same thing often happens in modern reactors, and there is no other reasonable explanation. The fact served as an added proof.

Finally, the French scientists announced their findings to the public. Four and possibly more natural reactors definitely existed at Oklo, Gabon, Africa, operating some 1.7 to 2 billion years ago. Moderated by groundwater, they produced energy off and on for about one hundred thousand years, creating enough heat to power several towns (if there had been towns at the time). The evidence was clear for every step in the process.

In the face of so many facts, no one could doubt that the natural chain reaction really happened. The Oklo Phenomenon, as Naudet calls it, is accepted as scientific truth.

Now, researchers are reexamining old and new uranium mines all over the world to see if the same phenomenon has happened in other places. It seems likely that it has. Finally, other researchers are studying Oklo, to see what can be learned about nature's safe and efficient method of storing nuclear waste underground.

Mining is going on again at Oklo, but the site of the second reactor found is being carefully preserved. Miners dig around and under it. The reactor site stays as a monument to the mysteries science still holds.

14 Death in the

Old Hotel

Tuesday, July 27, 1976

The mystery started slowly. An elderly man entered a Williamsport, Pennsylvania, hospital feeling tired, feverish, and short of breath. His doctor diagnosed pneumonia, complicated by heart trouble.

That night, the retired Air Force officer, whose hobby was collecting seashells, died. He had just returned, three days before, from an American Legion convention in Philadelphia.

Friday, July 30

In hospitals scattered across the state, four more men died of what was called pneumonia. The eldest was eighty-two; the youngest, thirty-nine. All four had attended the same American Legion convention.

Saturday, July 31

Dr. Ernest Campbell learned that three patients in his hospital, all with high fevers, congestion, chills, muscle aches, and other identical symptoms, had traveled together to an American Legion convention in Philadelphia. Now, all three were ill. Was there a connection?

Alarmed, he phoned the state Health Department's testing laboratory. It was closed for the weekend.

Meanwhile, in other hospitals, the mysterious malady killed six more Legionnaires. And most of the victims died horribly, gasping for breath and foaming blood from their constricted chests.

Sunday, August 1

Another patient died. Dozens of others were hospitalized. American Legion officers' telephones began buzzing with reports of sickness and death. Rumors flew.

The officers weren't sure what to do. Was it some kind of epidemic?

Monday, August 2

Dr. Robert Sharrar, chief of the Communicable Disease Control section of Philadelphia's Health Department, left his new town house and walked down Broad Street toward his office. On the way, he passed famous old Bellevue-Stratford Hotel, already busy with the morning crowd of Bicentennial tourists.

Dr. Sharrar opened the morning mail in his tiny, cluttered office and mused about the complications of the job ahead of him—immunizing everyone in Philadelphia against a possible swine flu attack. Suddenly, the telephone jarred his thoughts.

"We've had eleven deaths from pneumonia, and every case attended the American Legion convention last week," said Dr.

William Parkin, acting state epidemiologist.

Both men had the same thought. "Swine flu." An epidemic of the deadly influenza had been predicted for the coming winter, and Sharrar was making plans for mass inoculations. Now, it was probably too late.

Sharrar had a sinking feeling. If this killer pneumonia turned out to be swine flu, then the whole world might be in danger. As *The New York Times* later reported, Sharrar told Bill Parkin, "This is bigger than we can handle."

When a local police force needs special help, they call in the FBI. For help in this crisis, Dr. Parkin called in the CDC. The Center for Disease Control, located in Atlanta, Georgia, is a special government agency designed to handle all kinds of medical emergencies involving large groups of people.

Three epidemiologists from the CDC made plans to catch the next plane for Philadelphia. More followed.

Meanwhile, Sharrar and Parkin put all their emergency programs into effect. They alerted public health nurses, health inspectors, environmental engineers, and anyone else who might be able to help control the unknown killer. Action centered around the Bellevue-Stratford Hotel, just down the street from Sharrar's office. It was there that most of the ill-starred convention took place.

By noon, the press had learned about the epidemic. Radios and television broadcasts poured out disaster bulletins. For months, everyone in the country had been hearing about the dangers of swine flu. Now, all the dire predictions seemed to be coming true. The story made sensational news.

By late afternoon there were two more deaths. Other stricken conventioneers checked into hospitals. Most alarming of all, a health worker in Bill Sharrar's own office came down with the same symptoms. He had not been to the convention, but, like Sharrar, he often walked past the Bellevue-Stratford on his way to work.

Tuesday, August 3

Dr. David Fraser, from the CDC, arrived in Philadelphia with his team of trained epidemiologists. With Sharrar's help, Fraser took over. The investigation began to resemble preparations for war.

First, the team needed to find the agent causing the disease— if it *was* a disease. Every doctor treating the victims seemed to have a different theory: swine flu, typhoid, viral pneumonia, parrot fever. To find the answer, researchers dispatched samples of sputum, blood, urine, feces, and lung tissue to laboratories all over the state. More samples were flown to CDC head-quarters in Atlanta. Scientists in all those labs began searching the samples for signs of their own specialty: viruses, bacteria, or poisons.

Meanwhile, other researchers began hunting the next most important clue, the common denominator. If all the hundred or so cases of the mystery illness came from the same source, then every one of the victims must have come in contact, some-how, with that source. Nurses, doctors, technicians, and even policemen spread out and started interviewing Legionnaires, their families and friends, and other guests at several hotels, especially the Bellevue-Stratford.

"Did you attend the Keystone Go-Getters breakfast at the Bellevue-Stratford Hotel?" they asked.

"Did you use ice in your drinks?"

"Did you drink any water?"

"What restaurants did you visit?"

"Have you had any recent contact with pigs?"

Other "legworkers" interviewed the staff of hotels and restaurants in the area. "Have you been ill?" "Where do you buy your supplies?"

And always, "Have you had any recent contact with pigs?" This question was important because pigs sometimes harbor the dangerous swine flu virus.

Still others checked out the area. Air-conditioning systems are notorious for harboring bacteria. Workers collected samples of water and dust. Gratings in the street can provide a home for germs or poisonous fumes. They took more samples. Side street trees and even the nearby subway looked like possible dangers. More samples.

The scientists call this interviewing, questioning, and general snooping around the area of an epidemic "shoe-leather epidemiology," because of the hours of legwork it takes. Robert Sharrar even wears a silver lapel pin shaped like a shoe sole with a hole in it.

At temporary CDC headquarters in Harrisburg, Pennsylvania, David Fraser collected and coordinated the flood of information. His helpers set up a huge map of the state, to keep track of the spread of sickness. They stuck a red pin in it for every death. That day, nineteen red pins marked the towns where each victim had lived.

Seventy bright yellow pins scattered across the sheet indicated patients suffering from the mysterious symptoms. There were more than seventy cases by Tuesday afternoon, but the workers had run out of yellow pins. Fraser sent for more.

Still other workers manned a Hot Line for people who wanted to volunteer information or ask questions about the crisis. Sometimes, Hot Liners answered more than four hundred calls an hour.

Some callers offered advice. "I got a virus from a bottle of soda."

Or, "The Martians found a way to get back at us. This is their revenge." (A U.S. Viking spacecraft had landed on Mars just the week before.)

When Fraser and his staff began putting the first round of filled-out questionnaires together, they felt discouraged. They couldn't find a common denominator at all.

Some people had been to the special breakfast, but not every victim. A few drank water, but most did not. Most used some ice, but certainly not all. They ate in different restaurants, and almost no one had had any contact with pigs.

There was not even one single room every victim had been in, although almost all had passed through the lobby of the Bellevue-Stratford. After the questionnaires were tallied, the source was more of a mystery than ever.

Fraser ordered more questions. *Everyone* who had been to the convention had to be contacted, sick or well. Maybe the answer lay in what the healthy conventioneers didn't do, rather than what the stricken ones did. Legworkers set out again. A blitz of questionnaires went out by mail.

And a new scare came to light. Just when the scientists were feeling slightly glad to see that the fever did not seem to be spreading to families and friends at home, more cases from the local area began arriving. None of the new victims had been inside the Bellevue-Stratford Hotel, but they had all been along

Broad Street, within a block of the huge old building. Since the press was beginning to call the mysterious illness "Legionnaire's disease," they named the new set of cases "Broad Street pneumonia."

Meanwhile, at laboratories across the state and in Atlanta, work was moving as fast as possible—which isn't very fast. It takes time for virus or bacteria samples to grow.

At Children's Hospital, across town, Dr. Harvey Friedman's ninth floor virology lab worked late Tuesday night, skipping dinner. No one was very hungry. Testing samples that might contain a deadly virus is hard on the nerves.

In one section of the lab, the serum tests sat waiting. A microbiologist earlier in the day had mixed victims' red blood cells in saline (salt water) solution, with samples of known viruses. Tiny wells on plastic trays held A/Victoria flu, the most common flu "going around" in 1975. Another tray contained type B/Hong Kong flu, the killer from 1968. Finally, a tray of blood samples held the dreaded swine flu.

If a virus from any of those strains of influenza was causing the epidemic, antibodies in the victims' blood ought to clump up into particles big enough to see under an ordinary microscope in about twenty-four hours. So far, it was still too soon to check.

In a five feet-by-two feet tank, under a steel hood, sat rows of chicken eggs next to rows of labeled test tubes. The lab supervisor carefully pricked a hole in the top of each egg and added a tiny drop of tissue from one test tube into each egg, two eggs for each tube. If the tissue had been invaded by viruses, the viruses might grow in the eggs. But the growth would take several days, and the technique didn't always work. Some viruses just do not cooperate.

Now, the lab technicians were finishing the most delicate test of all. If the mysterious killer would not grow in eggs, it might grow in cultured cells. Cultured cells are animal cells grown in a lab.

The laboratory refrigerator held some carefully grown, expensive cultures. Dr. Friedman chose two. One was human; the other, monkey. This test took a week, but it might work if all the rest failed.

That evening, the radio reported more deaths from the unknown killer. There were no clues about the cause. "Whatever it is," said a scientist quoted in *Family Health*, "it's one of the most dangerous things in the world."

Wednesday, August 4

Interviewers recruited by Fraser's team carried their questionnaires to everyone in Pennsylvania who was involved in any way with the epidemic. They brought back more volumes of information to add to the huge chart Fraser was building at headquarters. But no new leads. The common denominator was still a mystery.

That morning, a young boy confessed a secret. He had thrown magician's smoke powder into the air-conditioning system of the old hotel a week before. Now, he was terrified that he had caused the disaster. Workers checked. The powder was harmless.

Bacteriological labs read their first tests and gave preliminary reports. No bacteria could be found.

Other labs, looking for a fungus, found nothing. And, so far, no traceable poisons. Every test seemed to come up negative.

In the virology labs at Children's and in Atlanta, it was time to read the first twenty-four-hour serum tests. But there was a problem. Normally, doctors take control samples as soon as the patient becomes ill, so that laboratory workers can compare them with the same patient's blood later in the disease. That way, they can spot and ignore anything that was present in the blood already.

But for these early tests, they had only one, late sample from each patient. So when Friedman bent over his microscope, he saw telltale clumps everywhere. Every victim had some anti-bodies against swine flu. Most had antibodies against A/Victoria, too. But what did it mean? Without control samples, it didn't mean much.

Harvey Friedman called the CDC virology lab in Atlanta, to compare notes. Dr. Gary Noble confirmed his worst fears. Yes, their samples showed positive for swine flu, too. But swine flu is similar to the killer flu that swept the world in 1918, and almost everyone over fifty years old has some antibodies to it floating in his or her blood. All but one of the victims was over fifty. The result: no proof, one way or the other.

Unfortunately, everyone wanted proof, and they wanted it fast. Politicians began demanding action. Newspaper reporters condemned scientists for not working hard enough. Some even began to suggest that the mysterious ailment might be the attack of a crazed human killer who was somehow managing to poison hundreds of people across Pennsylvania. Meanwhile, the death toll kept rising. Twenty-two people were dead.

By evening, Friedman decided to "harvest" some of the egg

samples. In other labs, virologists made the same decision. It was two days too early, but maybe something would show.

They chose five eggs. Carefully, the technician inserted a clean dropper into each egg. She sucked up some of the clear liquid and squirted it gently into a test tube. If there were live viruses in the sample, they would cause a red blob of cells to settle to the bottom of the tube. If not, the blood would float around in tiny pellets.

It took forty minutes for the cells to settle. The staff ate a pizza.

When the time was up, the whole team crowded into the lab. Someone opened the refrigerator. There, in neat rows, were all the samples. Every one was filled with red pellets. Every one was negative.

Had the reading simply been too early? Dr. Friedman checked with other labs. They all had the same answer. Negative.

Outside, it began to rain. Another victim died.

Thursday, August 5

At headquarters, a few facts were beginning to gel. Victims were still falling ill, still dying, but every one had come in some kind of contact with the lobby of the old hotel. Not a single family member or health worker had caught the disease—if it was a disease—from a victim. That meant the epidemic was not likely to spread around the state or around the world.

Another clue: almost no native Philadelphians came down with the malady. All but one or two of those who were ill were visitors to the city. But even though the lobby of the Bellevue-Stratford was the closest thing David Fraser could find to a common denominator, no hotel employee seemed to be sick. More than thirty people worked all day or all night in the possibly infected area, and they were all healthy. Dr. Fraser was positive all these were vital clues, but he couldn't quite put them together.

Meanwhile, five more victims died. The story was front-page news all across the country.

Friday, August 6

All the eggs tested negative, in Childrens', in Atlanta, and everywhere. So did the cell culture samples, even under an electron microscope. Swine flu would have grown in one or both.

So it wasn't swine flu. Sharrar and Fraser both felt relieved. A swine flu epidemic might have infected the world. But at least they would have known what they were fighting. Legionnaire's disease, whatever it was, was still a mystery.

Now, new theories flew wildly around. Some scientists were convinced the problem had to be ornithosis, a disease caused by bird droppings. The Bellevue-Stratford was a popular roost for pigeons. Others were equally convinced the trouble was a poison, escaping through the air conditioner or the water.

Some people suspected enemy sabotage. The army checked its biological weapons storage. Everything was safe.

Chemists and toxicologists analyzed everything victims might have touched. They could not find any trace of poison.

So far, twenty-seven people were dead from the epidemic. And 125 more patients lay in hospitals. More than three hundred health workers were still on the job, getting nowhere, and each lab report came back negative.

August 7-18

In the weeks that followed, the death count rose to twenty-nine and stopped. One hundred and eighty-two people were known to have caught the ailment. Most of them had attended the Legionnaire's convention, but several had come to the hotel for a Catholic Eucharist convention and a few for a candle-makers' gathering and a magicians' gathering. All had been in or near the Bellevue-Stratford.

Then, almost as suddenly as it began, the mysterious epidemic stopped. The scary headlines stopped, too, but the work went on. Scientists do not give up easily.

September, 1976

Dr. Sheila Katz, a Philadelphia pathologist, was one of the researchers still working on the mystery. She did some special tests on a piece of infected lung tissue. Then, two weeks later, she came down with the symptoms she had been studying. She lay ill for almost a month with unexplained pneumonia. Was it Legionnaire's disease? No one knew for sure.

November, 1976

Doctors held a luncheon at the Bellevue-Stratford Hotel to discuss progress. There wasn't very much to discuss. "We've ruled out essentially every suspect," said Fraser, as reported by *Newsweek*.

"It may be one year, five years, or a hundred years before our technology becomes efficient enough to cope with it," added Parkin.

The luncheon was the last ever held at the famous old hotel.

Panic had halted their business almost totally. Newspapers called the Bellevue-Stratford the "30th victim."

December, 1976

Meanwhile, in the red brick buildings in Atlanta, work went on. A microbiologist in the leprosy and rickettsia branch of the CDC had not given up on the idea that some sort of microbe caused the disease, even though every test had been negative. Joseph E. McDade was especially experienced at locating hard-to-find bacteria, because the lab in which he worked was designed to uncover just such organisms. Leprosy and rickettsia are both caused by unusual microbes, somewhere between viruses and bacteria.

McDade was looking at some old slides of lung tissue when he noticed something no one else had noticed. In one or two spots, the tissue slightly resembled tissue damaged by rickettsia. But all the rickettsia tests had been negative. He decided to try one more time.

McDade ground up frozen lung tissue from four of the Legionnaires who died and injected it into guinea pigs. The animals died. Then he injected tissue from the dead guinea pigs into chicken eggs. The egg embryos died.

For the first time, the deadly disease had been passed, in a lab, from one host to another and then another. Joseph McDade had done what no one else had been able to do. He had cornered the killer.

Dr. Charles C. Shepard, head of Dr. McDade's department, helped search for the tiny, almost invisible culprit. The two researchers transferred bits of egg yolks back into fluid taken from a survivor of Legionnaire's disease. Sure enough, antibodies

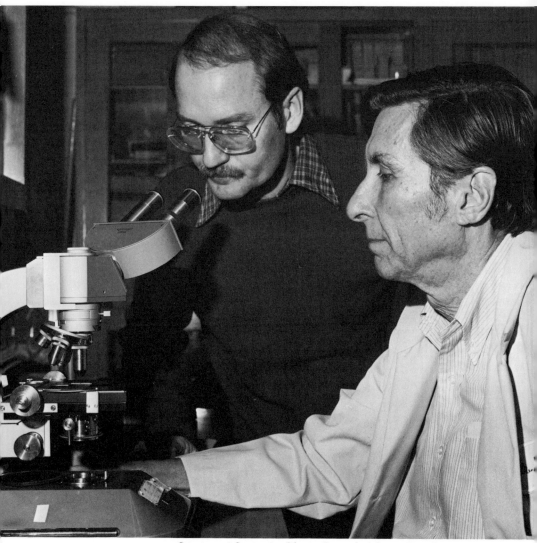

Joseph E. McDade (standing) and Charles G. Shepard, Chief of the
Leprosy and Rickettsia Branch, Center for Disease Control

in the fluid clumped around offending bacteria in the yolks. The first positive test! After six months of effort, McDade and Shepard had found the murderer.

"It's unlike anything we've ever seen before," said Shepard, in *Science News*. The mystery microbe stained pink, and it was rod-shaped and small, with pointed ends instead of the usual square or round.

January, 1977 (and on)

McDade's discovery opened the gates to a flood of new information. Far from being "new," the organism could be found—now that researchers knew how to look for it—in tissue samples saved from several curious crises in the past. In fact, one minor epidemic had happened at the same Philadelphia hotel, in 1974.

Researchers retested former employees of the now closed Bellevue-Stratford. Almost all had antibodies against legionosis (the new name for the disease) in their blood. They must have built up a slow immunity to the deadly disease, working in the old hotel.

No one yet knows for sure where the killer microbes lurked, or how and why they attacked their victims. But the Bellevue-Stratford was not the only source. *Legionella pneumophila* (the new name for the microbe) and close relatives have been found all around the world, from Europe to Australia, most often breeding in stagnant water. The elusive bacteria has turned out to be the culprit in dozens, probably hundreds of thousands, of unexplained illnesses, stretching back years into the past.

McDade and Shepard, the two CDC microbiologists, became the heroes of the story. But, like most modern scientific mysteries, they couldn't have solved it alone. Hundreds of people helped. Put together, all their efforts made a solution possible to what a former CDC director, in *The New York Times*, called "the greatest epidemiological puzzle of the century."

Index

(Page numbers in *italics* are those on which illustrations appear.)